CITIZEN SPY

Vatican Cover-Up:
The Mob, Money-Laundering and *Murder*

Robert W. Morgan

CITIZEN SPY

Copyright ©2010 Robert W. Morgan

All rights reserved. No portion of this book may be reproduced in whole or in part, by any means whatsoever, except for passages excerpted for the purposes of review, without the prior written permission of the publisher. For information, or to order additional copies, please contact:

TitleTown Publishing, LLC
P.O. Box 12093 Green Bay, WI 54307-12093
920.737.8051 | titletownpublishing.com

Cover design by Mike Stromberg
Interior layout and design by Erika L. Block
Edited by Julie Rogers

PUBLISHER'S CATALOGING-IN-PUBLICATION DATA:

Morgan, Robert W., 1935-
Citizen spy : Vatican cover-up, the mob, money-laundering and murder Robert W. Morgan. -- 1st ed. -- Green Bay, WI : TitleTown Pub., c2010.

p. ; cm.

ISBN: 978-0-9827206-0-8
1. Morgan, Robert W., 1935- 2. Undercover operations.
3. Money laundering investigation. 4. Mafia. 5. Mafia--Political aspects--Italy. 6. John Paul I, Pope, 1912-1978--Assassination. I. Title.

HV8079.M64 M67 2010 2010934521
363.25/968--dc22 1009

Printed in the USA by Thomson-Shore
first edition ♻ printed on recycled paper
10 9 8 7 6 5 4 3 2 1

CONTENTS

Acknowledgments   xi
Preface   xiii
Introduction   xvii

1. The Stalker   1
2. The Spook Test   16
3. Taxi!   29
4. My Fare Lady   37
5. The Rat's Nest   58
6. Freddy-Baby   69
7. Bonanno Decoded   78
8. The Unlikely Trio   87
9. From Moscow to East End Revelations   100

Afterword   127
Where Are They Now?   129
About the Author   131

ACKNOWLEDGMENTS

My first expression of gratitude belongs to my loving daughter. Without her unwavering love and support, I may not have achieved my goals, nor would I be half the person I have become. I certainly owe my survival to Agents Norman Jones and Fred Coward, with whom I remain close friends. I owe another huge debt to the memory of Frank Sturgis, a man I believe has been greatly misjudged by history. Without his friendship and counsel, I may not have survived Miami.

I also sincerely thank my agent, Stephanne Dennis, not only for her professional guidance, but also for her encouragement and friendship.

I can only hope this work encourages more parents to stand up and set a role model to their children with a "can do" attitude when it comes to protecting them from the evils of this world.

Lastly, I thank Alicia Dorey, from the bottom of my heart, for her unwavering support and influence; she made it all possible.

Pseudonyms replaced all children and certain innocent parties' real identities; however, wiseguys and their criminal pals are fair game.

What caring parent has not fantasized about taking serious revenge on those slimy drug pushers and their suppliers who prey upon children, even going so far as to enter the children's school playgrounds? **Citizen Spy** *is a thoroughly documented and corroborated account of one civilian father who did precisely that. His voluntary efforts helped cost the American Mafia more than half a billion dollars . . . and more, much, more.*

PREFACE

Citizen Spy is an extraordinary account narrated by an extraordinary man. Every parent whose child was ever exposed to illegal narcotics will appreciate what Robert W. Morgan accomplished as a father and private citizen. He materially assisted two federal agencies–the Federal Bureau of Investigation and the Drug Enforcement Agency–in an interagency operation, to uncover an unprecedented money-laundering scheme that directly involved Vatican officials.

During his career as a DEA agent and criminal investigator, Norman C.P. Jones handled hundreds of cases and presented expert testimony in numerous federal courts. In his thirty-plus years of law enforcement, Jones worked with hundreds of Confidential Informants ("CI's") to gain evidence that was beyond the reach of professional agents.

Virtually all CI's are criminals in their own right, cooperating only to serve their own interests. However, the CI Jones assigned the code name "Star" was no criminal. Instead, this civilian had been infuriated to discover drug dealers openly pedaling their poisons outside his daughter's schoolyard. Further enraged when the local police in South Florida brushed off his complaint, CI "Star" Morgan launched a personal investigation to gather evidence.

To accomplish this Morgan did the unthinkable. Using his reputation as a filmmaker, he ingratiated himself with key Mafia support figures by doing them small "favors." In a short time, he became so trusted that they invited him to move with them from Florida to Tucson, Arizona, to be close to the operation run by Joseph Bonanno, the capo di tutti capi or "boss of all bosses." Moreover, the Mafia proposed to build an entirely new film production studio for Morgan's projects as part of an elaborate scheme to import and launder the Mafia's illegally gained profits into the United States via his films. The scheme was only a small portion of the depth of money laundering and counterfeiting efforts surrounding him.

However, when Robert's daughter elected to live with him, he knew it was time to call for help. Jones was the lucky agent who answered Morgan's call, literally.

Frankly, every claim Morgan made during their initial interview seemed implausible; that is until Jones ran an intra-agency computer check on the names Morgan provided. To have a single federal case number per suspect pop up is sufficient to get serious attention, but when three popped up, Robert had that agent's full attention.

Jones was not alone in his astonishment by Morgan's chutzpah. Shortly after Jones filed a standard intra-agency query, FBI Special Agent Frederick Coward contacted him, wanting to know more about the report and this unique citizen CI. Coward's reputation as a top-flight FBI investigator was outstanding and he was a key player within a special task force specifically assigned to investigate Mafia crime boss Joseph Bonanno.

Under the combined aegis of both DEA and FBI, Morgan supplied a steady stream of invaluable intelligence that uncovered the most sophisticated money-laundering scheme in the history of international crime. Indeed, *Citizen Spy* lends credence to David Yallop's 1984 book, In God's Name: An Investigation into the Murder of Pope John Paul I, by providing the missing links behind the 1982 collapse of Italy's Milan-based Banco Ambrosiano and the deaths of its chairman Roberto Calvi ... and Pope John Paul I.

Just as astonishing, Robert uncovered the precise manner the Mafia used to secretly export and then import a reported half-billion dollars right under the Internal Revenue Service's nose.

Citizen Spy is not merely a retelling of Mafia events and involvements. While the story surrounds these things, it is only half of the compelling history. What makes this history complete is the motive of the author. As a common and ordinary citizen, how many people would be willing to go undercover among known criminals merely for the sake of doing what is right?

Would you?

INTRODUCTION

When I first listened to Morgan's story, I thought he was full of crap, yet he puzzled me when he offered to become a Confidential Informant (CI). After all, he wasn't just another criminal looking to weasel out of a personal problem by turning informant. Moreover, he wasn't anyone I would expect to be on the inside to serious criminal activity, yet he described them in intimate detail. Indeed, there was something about him that caused me check out his claims, and I am glad that I did; his was a story that truly amazed me and my FBI partner, Frederick Coward.

In the world of law enforcement, the usual CI is looking to reduce their prison sentence or carry out a personal vendetta, and it's not something anyone does for money. Hell, Morgan barely had his expenses covered while working with two federal agencies.

In the years that followed, Fred and I spent a huge amount of time with Robert, the CI I had dubbed "Star." Initially that tag was a somewhat snide swipe at his association with the film industry. However, we quickly grew to respect the work he did with us. After all, while being an average workaday guy, he risked his life to do what he thought was right.

Now that the most dangerous of those criminals we prosecuted have died and cannot pose a threat to him and his family, our Star is at last free to share his story–and an amazing story it is. It has action, it has humor, but in the end, it proves that good can prevail over evil.

Norman C.P. Jones
Retired Drug Enforcement Agent

# THE STALKER

It was too damn hot and too damn muggy for any sane man to be lurking about the playground of a primary school wearing a wig, tie-dye headband, cheap sunglasses, and a T-shirt advertising the back-street joys of Margaritaville. Certainly, no one who knew me would expect to see magnetic peace signs stuck on the hood of my new '74 Volkswagen Beetle, or crystal prisms, beads, and painted chicken feathers dangling from my rearview mirror.

However, despite my sweaty misery, I would be the happiest father in this Florida town if I could just score that day. My target was a young boy. Not just *any* boy, mind you; one, in particular, named Teddy. My daughter Emily's best friend Vicky advised me that Teddy was not handsome or even likeable really, but I wanted this brat on my radar scope in the worst way.

I intended to leave my North Miami office early enough to beat the worst of the traffic. I failed and the twenty-mile drive south was brutal. Bumper-to-bumper traffic clogged the Dixie Highway as frazzled office workers shuttled back to their look-alike suburban homes that were neatly stacked and packed in and around Kendall, Perrine, and all points south. Nevertheless, to make my mission to score a success, I had to be opposite a specific school before classes ended for the week.

Why?

Vicky had whispered that Fridays were when kids scored their weekend stash of weed, Quaaludes, LSD, cocaine, hash, speed, or whatever else turns their

CITIZEN SPY

little cranks.

In truth, what did I know about drugs, legal or illegal? The strongest stuff I took was an occasional aspirin.

Spotting a break in the traffic, I cut east, scooting over to snag a parking space within sight of the main entrance to the school.

I reassured myself for the umpteenth time that this was probably a dry run. Hell, kids tend to exaggerate, especially at age twelve. Maybe, at twelve, exaggerating life is part of growing up. I was sure my Emily's best friend was no different. However, my ears had pricked up when Vicky had whispered that every Friday, some runt in their class named Teddy bought drugs out of a beat-up old van to peddle to his classmates. I went on full alert when she added that everything took place in plain sight of their school.

Vicky also made me "pinky-swear" secrecy before whispering that Teddy always tries to push his junk on her and my Emily.

I truly hoped she was either wrong or exaggerating. Perhaps Teddy was swiping his mother's anti-depressants to play the big shot; or maybe that van belonged to an older brother and he was faking a buy. Either way, this stake out was today's mission. What parent wouldn't check out rumors like this in person, especially when said parent's pleas to the local cop shop had been sloughed off with a "so-what's-new" attitude?

I slid my VW to the curb, its engine mumbling to rest. My position was perfect. I had a clear view of the school entrance. I was in disguise. And with South Florida filled with anti-*everything* signs, symbols, and hippies, nothing about me would stand out, right?

Wrong.

One nosy neighbor waddled onto her porch to peer over at me. Luckily, before she decided to do a pervert check, the doors to the school blew open and a horde of screaming children swarmed out for another weekend of freedom. Some clambered into waiting buses while others scattered to parents' cars or vans.

Everything seemed normal enough until a battered white van with a broken, dangling driver's side mirror ground to a halt on the blind side of the nosy neighbor's house.

THE STALKER

I found it ironic that nosy woman was paying more attention to me than what was happening right under the nose she seemed fond of peering over. The scene behind nosy, regardless, was exactly as Vicky had described.

A scruffy brat with uncombed hair broke away from a cluster of look-alike street toughs, making a beeline to that van. In plain sight of anyone who looked, he removed a thick wad of something from his backpack and shoved it through the window at the driver. When he withdrew his hand, he was clutching a paper sack.

An eerie jolt of remembrance sent me flipping back through my memory bank. Out of the thousands of workaday white vans that plied South Florida streets, why did *this* one seem familiar? Was it that dangling mirror? My moment of speculation went on hold when Emily and Vicky appeared directly opposite my parking place. *Crap!* Their path could bring them directly in front of me! Would my ridiculous disguise work? If Emily caught me, what excuse could I offer for spying?

Fate struck again when ratty-tatty Teddy "saved the day" by offering Emily and Vicky a peek into his newly purchased bag of tricks. Thankfully, my girls rushed away, from me and from the peddling Teddy, crossing the street behind me before I could jerk my car door open and blow the entire gig by assaulting a minor.

But Teddy did not miss a beat; his gang of punks was already mobbing him, peeking into his bag of goodies.

I didn't understand. Where were the police? Where were the SWAT teams, detectives, sirens, paddy wagons, paratroopers, attack helicopters, and gangs of pissed-off parents armed with a rail and plenty of hot tar and feathers for that van driver? These are our children! They depend on us for guidance, for protection, and we have a sacred vow to keep them safe!

I ranted in my head, getting angrier and more frustrated by the moment. A passing conversation interrupted my mental rant.

"Look at that Teddy go, man! He's really hooked up tight," bragged a gangly boy in a red shirt. "He can score *anything*. He's one cool dude, man."

"Far out," cooed a scrawny girl dressed in a bright yellow blouse.

"He gets the best grass, man," Red Shirt went on. "It's primo buds; no leaves or stems or that other crap. Ditch weed is so uncool. He even has all the 'ludes and speed you'd ever want. Ever try it?"

"Try what?" Yellow Blouse asked.

"'Ludes,"

"Would I cop a buzz?" she asked.

"Get real! They'll make you so mellow all you wanna do is get it on."

"Gimme a break," sneered a chubby girl following close on their heels.

"I'll spring for 'em if you'll take 'em," Red Shirt said to Yellow Blouse.

"Nuh-uh, I can't. My old man really pitched a fit the last time I partied with you."

"How will he know? My old lady already split for the weekend so we're cool at my pad. I even swiped some of her boyfriend's Trojans. We could have a blast."

My mind reeled at the content of the conversation. I forced myself to focus on listening rather than letting my fatherly tendency take root and start lecturing these seemingly lost kids.

"I-I dunno. I've never done that. My dad would kill me," Yellow Blouse said while Chubby Girl promised to be there at eight o'clock sharp.

Mind still reeling, I thought perhaps I should make a grab for Teddy's supplier. Surely, that nosy neighbor would call the law when she saw me wrapping my "just in case" axe handle around the supplier's throat to make a citizen's arrest? I looked around for the van and was almost too late. Whoever he was, he was nearly out of sight.

I cranked my Bug awake, ramming her into gear, and peeling out in pursuit. Finally free from nosy's prying eyes, I ripped off my itchy wig, swatted those dangling gewgaws off my mirror, and settled into a game of follow-the-leader as the white van shot back across the Dixie Highway on a course running due west.

My mind raced. What to do? I knew I would lose my prey if I paused to call the cops. Besides, what would I say? I had not seen nor could I identify exactly what they exchanged, and I certainly had no proof that Teddy had anything illegal

THE STALKER

in his bag. Perhaps that driver really *was* his brother. For all I knew, it was only a bag of baby aspirins or No-Doz.

I snapped at myself mentally to *stop making excuses*. I saw what I saw, I heard what I heard, and the whole situation was a damned serious one. I had to stay focused; I had no other option.

My quarry banked a sudden right turn into the parking lot of the popular Monkey Jungle tourist park. I made a quick U-turn to park where I had a decent view of the entire parking lot. I leaped out to remove those peace signs from my hood transforming my Bug into just another plain old VW. I hopped back into my car and watched a short, swarthy man with thick black hair leave a new Porsche convertible and approach the van.

Unlike the common snowbird *turista*s who sport flowery Bermuda shorts and bright Hawaiian shirts, this guy wore sharply pressed linen slacks, a crisp Cuban-style guayabera dress shirt, and windshield sunglasses; only his polished black briefcase spoiled his relaxed cool. When he snapped it open, the scruffy van driver deposited a thick wad of something in it.

The sharp-dressed one snapped the case shut, spun on his heel, and swaggered back to his car. I scribbled his license plate numbers onto a scrap of paper as the van spun out to resume its course due west, straight toward the edge of the Everglades.

I was stuck. I wasn't sure what to do or, if I kept following, who to follow. *Make up your mind, Morgan: do you follow the Porsche or the van?*

Who was I kidding; the Porsche's driver looked like someone who considered speed signs a challenge and I doubted my Bug could keep up no matter how hard I tried.

A second U-turn placed me some seventy-five to a hundred yards behind the van. If I was lucky, the van driver was slack-jawed and stupid and wouldn't notice me. Then it dawned on me that maybe he already had. Perhaps he was deliberately drawing me into the Everglades where hundreds of square miles of nothingness were home to hungry alligators, snakes, and bone-picking vultures.

To stay on the safe side, I retrieved my palm-sized, High Standard .22-magnum derringer, which I affectionately dubbed "Maggie May or May Not," from its hiding place. Maggie May was my safety net, assuring me that any bad guy would have the choice of retreating or accepting a two-boom hollow-point salute. Yes, of course, it was illegal, but so is robbery and assault and I was willing to take my chances.

My target and I continued due west until we dead-ended at Krome Avenue, a long and lonely road that marked the easternmost edge of the wild Everglades. Perhaps the remote location was getting to me, but it seemed that driver was pausing far longer than necessary. Was he studying me through his good mirror? Maybe he was only rolling a joint. No matter, I made a show of holding up a map and staring right, left, right, left. I nearly got whiplash before the he finally made a right turn to proceed north.

Naturally, I turned south and sped away until he was out of sight before reversing direction. I barely had him back in my sight before he took a sharp left, vanishing behind a wall of thick tropical undergrowth. I kept my eyes glued on that exact spot of his turn but intentionally swept past only to receive a second jolt from my memory. That veil of palmetto bushes he punched through rang a bell. As implausible as it seemed, I recognized that specific lane as a spider-like tunnel, soft and treacherous, tangled with vines, and wild as hell.

By coincidence, a year or more before I had traipsed the entire length of that lane with Laymond Hardy, a local expert on tropical flora and fauna whose hobby was collecting rare tropical orchids and colorful tree snails sold to him by those whom he called "backwater swampies." I had accepted his invitations to tag along as often as possible because any field trip with that walking, talking encyclopedia of obscure science was an adventure.

As I recalled, that lane ended amid a cluster of shacks inhabited by a pair of skinny, rotten-toothed squatters straight out of the film *Deliverance*. Indeed, when Hardy and I had arrived, we discovered the gangly male standing beside that same white van squeezing his pimples into its dangling mirror. The mental picture flooded my memory with disgusting clarity.

I remembered a dilapidated house trailer surrounded by a storage shed, a poor imitation of a Seminole chickee, an outhouse, a weedy vegetable garden, and *mounds* of trash heaped around the rusting shell of an ancient school bus. I

THE STALKER

also remembered Hardy whispering that the people we were about to encounter were hardcore druggies with deep-fried brains. Druggies or not, they provided him with rare wild orchids and his precious tree snails, all illegally harvested for a price, of course.

Indeed, that ultra-skinny male had ambled over to greet us while his hollow-cheeked girlfriend emerged to offer us warm brownies. One nibble and I discovered a serrated leaf; I palmed the leaf and ditched the remainder of the brownie under my seat.

I mulled this revelation over while continuing north, well past the lane the van turned onto, but did not dare touch my brake pedal. It was an even-steven chance that the scumbag might be watching; besides, I needed time to think. Obviously, there was no longer any doubt in my mind that he was supplying drugs to my daughter's schoolmates.

My brow furrowed with determination. Damn it, if the cops didn't have time to stop him, then I did.

But how? Who was I? I was no crime fighter. I was just a normal guy. I had my hands full trying to establish myself as a screenwriter and freshman film director. Along with my partners Ben Morse, Irv Rudley, and Stan Webb, we had recently barely scraped together enough money to produce *Bloodstalkers*, our first feature-length film, due for release in a few months.

Once again, I found myself having an argument in my head. With hopes of larger productions looming, part of me said I should stick to business. Why get personally involved? Perhaps I could write something that would portray this situation and, and, and . . . *bull crap!* My Emily and her friends and classmates were being *stalked* every Friday after school and would continue to be unless... unless what?

My mind was shifting into hyper-drive as I pulled into the convenience store at the junction of Krome Avenue and the Tamiami Trail. I knew I had to keep in mind that I was meeting that very evening with Frank Sturgis, the recently paroled Watergate burglar.

We intended to explore the media potential of his adventures as a covert CIA contractor embedded within Fidel Castro's Cuban Revolution in the early

1960s. According to him, the CIA had assigned him to assassinate Castro if or when the Oval Office issued an official sanction, aka his death warrant. Made impatient by President John F. Kennedy's waffling, Sturgis and his compadres, Pedro and Marcos Diaz Lanz, had tried to kill Castro three times, but failed to do the dastardly deed before they were forced to flee to the safety in the United States. Unfortunately, a Congressional committee ignored their testimony.

I slugged coins into a public telephone, the only option back then, and dialed my office. Mitzi Rudley, our expert film editor, answered in a hurried tone.

"Creative Film and Sound; how may I help you, please?" she panted.

"Schedule me for a brain transplant. Is Frank Sturgis there yet?"

"Oh, thank God, Robert! He just called. He can't get here until five-thirty or maybe six."

"Would you stay long enough to let him in, pretty-please? I'm way south and the traffic is a bitch."

"I'm still editing your Bakir perfume commercial for Germaine Montiel. They're going to love it! But once I tuck him in, I'm going home or I'll go blind!"

"OK, but please ask Frank to take a look at that book proposal I'm drafting. It's on my desk. And what do you think of my title: *Secrets from the Sturgis Files?"*

"Oh, I love it! And guess who Frank's bringing with him? Oscar Fraley! And he said Eddie Egan might meet you both later! Isn't that exciting? All these famous people!" she gushed.

I wracked my brain. Oscar Fraley was a former UPI sports writer and best-selling author, known for his work with crime buster Eliot Ness. His book, *The Untouchables,* sold 1.5 million copies and was the basis for the television series and movie of the same name. I found out later that he was finishing *Hoffa: The Real Story* when we met.

"Yeah, right. So remind me, who's Eddie what's-his-name?"

"Good God, Robert! Mr. Egan is that New York detective who made the biggest heroin bust in New York *history*! *The French Connection* is already listed as one of the top films ever made and it won an Academy Award! I just love Gene

THE STALKER

Hackman. Didn't you see it?"

"Er, yeah, but I didn't memorize it."

"Maybe Mr. Fraley is getting involved because he's already working on Frank's stuff. I am so excited!"

"Gotta run, Mitzi . . . "

"Oh, and the McDermott Casting Agency called to say some TV people in LA are asking if some treatment is finished. What's that about?"

"I'd read in the *Hollywood Reporter* that Quinn Martin Productions is looking to do a crime thing in Miami, so I sent them a one-page concept. They liked it and asked for a full treatment. I told them I'd get back to them in a few weeks and gave them Beverly's name as a contact."

"What's your story about?"

"Mitzi, I really gotta jet."

"But I am staying late just for you!"

"It's about a Cuban refugee in Miami who'd been Havana's top detective before Castro took over. Since he can't join any police force until he's a naturalized citizen, he hacks cabs to stay alive until he gets his papers. As a cabbie, he sees lots of crap going down on the streets and pitches in to help the Miami Police Department solve crimes. Kiss-kiss, Mitzi. Gotta go." I smiled as I put the receiver back in the cradle.

I jumped back in my car to think. Should I go back to that drug dealer's hovel and . . . do what? I didn't know what to do. The only thing I *did know* was I had a choice; the moment and the mood were mine to seize or to lose forever. Which would it be? Was I a man-father or a mouse-father?

I returned to the obscure lane where the van had turned, and carefully and quietly backed my Bug in until the palmetto bushes folded shut over the hood. After all, I might not have time to turn around should I need to "exit stage left" in a hurry.

What was my plan? I had no plan other than confronting this bastard and letting him know there are parents on this earth who will *not* idly stand by while criminals like him sell poison to their children or any other child.

Who was I kidding? There was no reasoning with him or any of his ilk, and

CITIZEN SPY

I knew it. I milled around my car, thinking. I grabbed my briefcase with work papers from the seat to stash in the trunk. I had a pleasant surprise when I opened the trunk and discovered my old drag-bag stuffed with a tattered camouflage jumpsuit; slouch hat; green, black, and tan facial grease paints; and a pair of jungle boots that I used when I roamed around the 'glades in the hopes of catching a glimpse of what they called Bigfoot. Omen? Divine intervention? Regardless of what some may see it as, I took it as a sign.

When I was fully suited up and greased, I tucked Maggie May into my hip pocket, retrieved my resident axe handle from its resting place behind my car seat, and slipped into the tropical underbrush. Guided by the sound of a sputtering generator, I was less than twenty yards out when my target emerged from his trailer to look around.

"Darlene? Where the hell are ya?" Skinny Man yelled. "That batch yer cookin' is 'bout ready, so don't be fuckin' it up. I got that shit sold to some tweakers tonight." I strained my mind to translate the lazy, drawling dialect.

A woman's voice screeched something unintelligible before the outhouse door slammed open and a hag, presumably Darlene, emerged while hitching up her filthy jeans.

"Goddam-sum bitch, don't be yellin' at me when I'm takin' a dump! Now you got my guts all tight again and I won't shit for a week!"

I hunkered down further to blend in among a patch of fan palmetto bushes while Skinny approached a weathered picnic table crowded with rusting lanterns, empty beer bottles, and used plastic plates. He cleared a section with a sweep of one skinny arm, withdrew wads of bills from his pockets, and commenced sorting them.

"Here, lemme help," Darlene said. "You can't count for shit."

"Jus' git yer ass in-nair to mind that stove! One of these days yer gonna blow us clean to hell!"

"Who's buyin' t'night?" she asked.

"Some college kids wanna try some good shit; they've got big bucks so I'm gonna hook 'em up good."

I could not believe my ears. This *creature*—he could *not* possibly be a human

THE STALKER

being—was about to infect naive kids looking for cheap thrills without realizing how easily it was to become addicted for life. It was at that precise moment that I appreciated the legal defense term "temporary insanity."

I felt a rush of white-hot adrenalin flooding every cell of my body and brain. Was it mere adrenalin or sheer hatred? This was the real deal and those wrinkled bills he was pawing through represented missed lunches by hungry kids, allowances, and nickels, dimes and quarters scraped together by mowing lawns, washing cars, or flipping burgers. How much of it, too, had been stolen from trusting parents only to be squandered to buy poisons that brought doom, destruction, and despair in exchange for fleeting moments of phony pleasure?

I moved without thinking, my body reacting to sheer emotion.

The woman spotted my camouflaged form first when I arose from the underbrush. Her scabby lips formed words that her closed throat could not utter. Realizing she was speechless, she scrambled to the trailer, slamming shut the door and snapping the lock, leaving the oblivious Skinny to Maggie May and me.

"What the hell bug went up yer ass, woman . . . Oh, m'gawd! W-who are you? Whatchu want? We got business? You buyin'?" Skinny stuttered when he finally noticed me.

"Hey, you cain't rob me, man; you don't know who yer fuckin' with! Call Mikey Ducks—did he send you? If I shorted him t'day, it was an accident! I don't do that to Mikey, I swear by my Lord Jesus Christ and the Holy Virgin!" he rambled.

"You've just peddled your last bag of poison to kids, you soulless bastard," snarled someone seemingly using my voice.

"W-what? *Fuck you!* What's it to you?! Wait-wait! Was one of those little fuckers yours? Who are you, mannnn?" Skinny implored.

"Just one pissed off papa, *mannnnn*."

"OK, OK! I-I only do what I'm told! I'm sorry! Your kid made a bad buy? Here, take it back," he stammered, pitching bills at me with one hand while tugging at the locked trailer door with the other. He must have seen the glint of insanity in my eye.

CITIZEN SPY

He turned and yelled, "Darlene! Open the door, you bitch! Get my gun; shoot this sucker and we'll feed his ass to the motherfuckin' 'gators! *Shit!*"

Wham! A whiz-miss by my axe handle sent him dancing and prancing back toward his van. Fumbling with the van's sticky door, he bellowed, "Mikey Ducks'll have your ass on a platter! He works for Butch Piazza, for chrissake! Butch'll kill you! He's the Main Man down here! You don't wanna mess with Atlanta! Darlene! Get my gun, bitch! *Shoooooot 'im!*"

My right arm lifted on its own accord to point Maggie May directly at his twisted face. At the last moment, with the very last one-hundredth of a second left to spare before I fully squeezed the trigger, something inside me screamed *NO!* I veered off target, firing —c*raaaack!*— *and* the van's window exploded all over the skinny, dancing man.

Perhaps he could not see my tiny palm-sized weapon or perhaps his fuzzed-up brain presumed that blast had come from some magical fingertip. Either way, Skinny dived between two palmetto scrubs to disappear into the surrounding undergrowth.

It mattered not one whit to me because my mind and emotions flat-lined. I was neither cold nor hot; I was on some sort of a primordial fight-or-flight autopilot. His flight merged instinct with fury to make me into the perfect hunter. I paused and actually sniffed air made sour by his sweating fear; it conjured not an ounce of pity. Instead, it keened my desire to hunt him down and cause his bitter end. After all, less than an hour before I had watched his poisons offered to a child for whom I would give my very soul. Now this creature was alone with me in the wilds of a vast, lonely, savage place that had not changed since time began.

Yes, I admit I fleetingly considered this was not the course our overly civilized legal system would follow, but where in hell was that sanctimonious system when my Emily's school let out? I took my time, replacing Maggie's spent cartridge with a spare round, and retrieved my axe handle.

Skinny's was an easy track to follow; he had left a highway of freshly smashed foliage. My ears honed in to a sound and I strained to listen. Somewhere ahead I heard him moaning about being so sorry (man), that it was all a mistake (man), and that he would never *ever* short Mikey Ducks or Butch again (man).

THE STALKER

He still didn't get it, that I wasn't some drug pusher but rather a pissed off parent. But why had he stopped running? I slowed my steps, creeping forward until I emerged from the head-high foliage to stand less than ten yards from my quarry.

Did I smile or laugh aloud at his dilemma?

Skinny's escape path had disappeared into a long, swampy pond hemmed by thick walls of razor-sharp saw grass. Thank God, my Miccosukee Indian friends had taught me well. When I slid my fingers upward along the saw grass's slender blades, there was no problem; however, if I reversed direction it immediately drew blood. Tough stuff, but saw grass was not my quarry's only problem. Oh my, no. This particular pond was home to something far more ominous. Lining the banks was a gang of huge, toothy, and definitely unfriendly alligators.

I spoke to Skinny in the rawest of back-alley terms, knowing only that could penetrate his primitive skull. Either his days of peddling poisons around schoolyards were permanently over or I would "tippy-tip, bap-bap" that message into his skull, collarbone, arms, legs, and both feet using axe-handle-style Braille. If *that* didn't sink in, I might need to resort to violence.

Skinny screamed back that I would be stupid to so much as muss his stringy hair. Didn't I know that he worked for the most powerful Mafia crew in Florida? Didn't I know that even if I killed him, someone else would take his place before sunrise?

We stood staring at one another, each knowing that all our tomorrows were about to be determined. On one hand, I could smack him into alligator bait in less than a dozen heartbeats and those resident gators would crunch him stem-to-stern and cache his parts below the waterline for a rainy-day snack.

Then it hit me, damn it; it would be wrong in too many ways to cork him off. After all, even this disgusting creature was someone's child. Moreover, he had spoken a solemn truth. His disappearance would have zero effect on drugs dealt to kids all around America or the world. To make a dent in this madness, I must make my war against those who made the real profits. My mind railed. *Say what? Am I nuts?* I was a neophyte filmmaker and the world sure as hell did *not* need another vigilante! But what else could I do, damn it, if I truly wanted to protect my daughter and more kids like her?

Unsure of my next act, I turned away. However, Skinny made a life-changing decision when he misread my action and bellowed after me, "Hey, fuck-head! Stay away from me from now on, man! I'm gonna peddle my shit anywhere I damned well want and that includes to your shit-ass kid, understand? Next time I see your ass, you'll be dealing with Mikey Ducks and Butch."

Icy-cold hit me again. I whipped back around to lift my right hand, only to point my finger at him. With the distance between us there was no way he could tell if it was just a finger . . . or more.

"Unless you walk on water, you son of a bitch . . ." I yelled.

A loud splash was all that followed. Perhaps he recalled his van's window exploding the last time I had lifted that hand. Whatever his reasons, Skinny took a flying flop into that alligator pond and began thrashing toward the opposite shore, some thirty-odd yards distant. My mouth went as dry as a Mississippi cotton ball when the gang of alligators hurled themselves, en masse, into the water behind him like a pack of warty water-wolves. Worse, the largest and most powerful of the group submerged beneath Skinny with a great whip of its tail.

I shouted warnings over and again, but my voice was lost amid his own string of vile curses. From behind me, a huge explosion rang out. I spun around as a ball of orange flames and angry smoke spewed up from the clearing behind me. Leaving Skinny to whatever fate had in store, I raced pell-mell back along the path to discover the house trailer enveloped in orange flames and black smoke. Sprinting through the holocaust toward my Beetle, I noted that the white van had disappeared, as had the remnants of cash Skinny left scattered on the picnic table.

I fired up my car's engine and blew out through the thin, green curtain, barreling north as fast as the Bug's little tires could spin.

As the miles peeled away, my initial shock faded into a morbid satisfaction. I realized I wanted to do more; that nickel-and-dime operation behind me was nowhere near as important as that slick-haired character in that new Porsche. What had he called him? Mikey Ducks? OK, so my mission now was to find him and light a fuse, blowing him and his bosses to Hell where they could join their

THE STALKER

pal Skinny.

My rational side tried to kick in again. Who was I kidding? To get to them I'd need the counsel of an expert in the art of spying, covert warfare, sabotage, and who knew what else! Ironically, Frank Anthony Sturgis fit that description perfectly, and I would be nose-to-nose with him within the hour.

My heart leaped as I saw a Florida state trooper, lights flashing and siren screaming, come skidding around the corner of Krome Avenue and Tamiami Trail, racing south toward the pillar of smoke growing distant in my rearview mirror.

Hmmm.

I wonder if he noticed that I was smiling.

THE SPOOK TEST

I bounded up the steps to my second-floor office to find Frank Sturgis ensconced in my chair with his size-twelve-triple-wide shoes propped up on my desk. He had not only scattered my neatly drafted proposal in every which direction, but I also caught him in the act of dropping *another* cigarette butt into my personal coffee cup.

I opened my mouth to pitch a fit but he cut me off, snapping that my tardiness had put off Oscar Fraley's attendance. Apparently, we would be meeting some dude named Egan later that evening, instead.

He flipped a private note from Mitzi in my general direction, his too-innocent look announcing that he had read every word. I snatched up the note, giving his cavalier grin a sideways glare. Her message told me that moments after our conversation, Quinn Martin Productions called from Los Angeles to request six episodic synopses about my Cuban cab driver/detective concept. Great news, except I didn't know diddlysquat about driving a taxi. Now, with my mind already reeling from everything suddenly happening in my world, I would have to wheedle a night job hacking for a couple of weeks to get the feel for taxi driver action and lingo.

However, at the moment, I cared nothing about make-believe stuff surrounding my livelihood. I had to focus on other things first. Topping my list:

THE SPOOK TEST

asking Frank's advice about how to remove every drug pusher who might appear at my daughter's schoolyard.

I flopped onto the couch, pretending to pay attention to his critique of my draft proposal. My mind, instead, began flipping back to my first encounter with this legendary bad-boy. Only a few short months had passed since he had burst into my office, demanding I become both his biographer and screenwriter. I was equally complimented and baffled. Baffled because I wasn't sure why he was asking *me*. Up to then my work had been limited to low-budget screenplays and a few TV concepts.

I expressed my confusion. No problem, Frank had said, seeming to know all about me. My end of the deal was limited to grunt work while he had already convinced oft-published Oscar Fraley to do the final polish. Together we three would shop for a publisher.

Sturgis' rules of engagement were specific: I could take notes on all he said but there must be no recorders, no third-party witnesses, and interviews must take place behind locked doors or in any other place of *his* choice. Our meetings would not be formally scheduled but, rather, spontaneous and at his discretion. Moreover, my notes must remain under lock and key.

Everything about the interaction reiterated that he would be perfect to help me in my new "hobby." I had agreed, signed a contract, and my education began. This "education" was what I relied on in making my decision to convince Frank to mentor me.

I learned that at the tender age of seventeen, Frank became a private in Lieutenant Colonel Merritt A. Edson's highly decorated 1st Marine Raider Battalion. Having lied about his age to the recruiter, Sturgis celebrated his eighteenth birthday blasting Japanese snipers out of palm trees in the South Pacific's Solomon Islands. Somehow, he also managed to survive the invasions of Tulagi, Guam, and Guadalcanal's infamous battle at Bloody Ridge.

At the close of World War II, similar to many returning combat veterans, Frank had a rough time adjusting to civilian life. During a brief stint as a rookie police officer in Philadelphia, he received a reprimand for shooting at an armed suspect who was fleeing the scene of a crime. This made no sense to Sturgis:

the suspect was a bad guy who refused to halt, so shoot the son of a bitch. The crook has civil rights? So do honest civilians, and Sturgis had made a decision to shoot.

The police chief did not agree, so Frank told him to shove his badge and he enlisted in the U.S. Army. At least there, he believed, taking down bad guys earned praise, medals, and promotions rather than scorn and reprimand.

The Army assigned him to an intelligence unit in Germany during the dangerously tense Berlin Airlift when America faced down the Soviet Union for domination. The Kremlin wanted all of Berlin and every yard of Eastern Germany while the Free World demanded at least half of Berlin and the entire West.

Frank was back at home among kindred-spirited soldiers. Their assignment: to hold at bay any Soviet invasion until Allied troops mobilized for a counteroffensive. Quickly elevated to the rank of sergeant, he became a clerk with a Secret clearance. He did fine until he fell in love with a young woman who convinced him that she was another helpless and hungry refugee needing his manly kindnesses. Feeding his vanity, she became inquisitive about his work, work that gave him access to Army secrets. Blinded by passion and woefully inexperienced with the opposite sex, Frank had no clue that his purported fiancée was an undercover Israeli *Shai* agent for the *Haganah,* a Jewish paramilitary organization, and milking him for every possible detail. Worse, he discovered she was also his commanding officer's mistress.

Thoroughly disgusted with life in general and betrayed by love, Sturgis accepted a second honorable discharge and returned to the States. This time, however, he was hell-bent on high adventure. Using every penny of his savings and all that he could borrow from family and friends, he rescued a World War II Martin B-26 Marauder bomber from a scrap heap, launching a new career as a freelance mercenary in the causes of freedom. Whose freedom? Any freedom-loving son of a bitch who could pay the freight, that's who!

Destiny stepped in when Frank's first customers were Fidel and Raul Castro whose ragtag band of revolutionaries was struggling to overthrow Cuban Dictator Fulgencio Batista. Fidel quickly discovered the gutsy Yankee was precisely who they needed on their side. Time after time, Frank's wave-skimming, radar-dodging

THE SPOOK TEST

night flights between Florida and the foothills of the Sierra Maestra Mountains, Cuba's largest mountain range, delivered food, medicine, arms, and munitions to postage-stamp airstrips slashed into remote sugarcane fields.

Moreover, while Frank was earning Castro's respect and gratitude, he was also making the "A" list for recruitment by Central Intelligence Agency back in the States.

Jan. 1, 1959: Batista resigned and fled Cuba. Havana fell to the rebels, led by Fidel Castro. In appreciation for his aid, Fidel appointed Sturgis his sole representative to all the casinos and hotels still controlled by the American Mafia (*La Cosa Nostra,* or "our thing"). In Castro's mind, he was the perfect *paisano* who understood their culture, values, and *modus operandi*. In addition, he placed Frank in charge of security for Cuba's air force under his compadre, Colonel Pedro Diaz Lanz.

However, the Castro brothers chose that moment to reveal their closely held secret that they despised all forms of democracy, most especially American style. Worse, the Castros not only granted the Soviet Union a military toehold in the Western Hemisphere, they were prepared to import nuclear-tipped intercontinental ballistic missiles (ICBMs) to point at America.

Realizing this second betrayal of his trust, Sturgis and the Lanz brothers–Pedro and Marcos–leaped into the arms of CIA, begging their sanction to assassinate these two tyrants. The CIA's response was that only a "sitting president" could authorize that sanction, and President Kennedy was not so inclined.

The political doublespeak held no excuse to Frank or his compadres, so they tried three times to kill Fidel, with each plot falling short. Finding themselves under suspicion by Fidel's secret police, and knowing the Castros' medieval methods of extracting information, the three freedom fighters fled to the United States.

Their problems did not end as they had hoped. A Select Congressional Committee ignored Pedro Diaz Lanz's testimony until Oct. 28, 1962, when the Cuban Missile Crisis brought America and the Soviet Union within literal moments of a nuclear war neither could survive.

As I mulled over all I had learned about Frank, aligning him mentally to become a new mentor, his bark yanked me back to the present.

"What the hell, Morgan! Do you agree or not?" Frank fumed.

"What? Oh, sure, sure . . ."

"You're acting like you're a mute. Who the hell am I talking to, a brick wall?"

"Hey, Frank, I'm in with all you said and I'll take action, but just now I need a favor," I said as I flipped him the scribbled note with Porsche-boy's license plate numbers. "I need to know who this guy is and where I can find him,"

"Why?"

"I saw a dealer who's been pushing drugs at my daughter's schoolyard pay off this guy out at Monkey Jungle; he's driving a new Porsche. I followed him into the Everglades and, well, um . . . stuff happened."

"Tell me you didn't follow the Porsche!" he growled.

"I knew I couldn't keep up, so I took off after the dealer's van and followed him. Then when I saw where he was going I realized I'd seen him before."

"So what 'stuff' happened?" he asked.

"Er, well, I'm pretty sure he's out of business . . . permanently."

Frank's face lost all expression but his eyes hardened. "Take it from the get-go, Bobby, and don't leave a single thing out; if you do, our deal is over."

His expression did not change the entire time I spoke. I included everything from the pay-off in the parking lot to the explosion leading to my hasty exit stage left.

He sniffed twice, grunted, and leaned closer. "Now describe the guy driving the Porsche."

I barely completed a single sentence before his feet hit the floor with a thud.

"Was Mitzi here when you came in?" he snapped.

"Er, no."

"Make sure she's not in the building!"

Confused, I ran down the hall to her editing room and then charged down the steps. Seeing no one, I ran back up.

"She's gone."

THE SPOOK TEST

"Does she use drugs?"

"No way."

"What about your partner, Irv-what's-his-name."

"Rudley? Maybe prescription stuff for nerves."

"What about that other guy, Stan what's-his-name?"

"Stan Webb is a good guy."

"That's not my question," he barked.

"I, uh–he's a musician, right? He lives in Miami, right? Every time I see him he's wiping his nose."

"So what does that tell you?"

"I've seen lines of snow now and then, but he's really a great guy. He only does that when he's recording all night."

"Listen up! Never trust anyone who shoves snow up their nose or hits the needle. They can't help themselves."

"OK, OK. Sorry," I stammered.

"Did anyone know where you went today?"

"No."

"You're 100 percent sure?"

"Yes. I'm sure. I even sneaked a wig and some hippy stuff out of our prop room in my briefcase–what're you doing?"

Snapping his cigarette lighter to flame, he destroyed the note with the Porsche's license number.

"Ever hear the name Meyer Lansky?" he asked.

"Who hasn't," I sighed. "He just got acquitted of all those charges of money laundering for the Mafia. They never so much as laid a glove on him."

"How about Frank Costello?"

"Big-time Mafia don. Retired, I think. He was tight with Lucky Luciano and became part of The Commission after they killed off Salvatore Maranzano for trying to play the big shot," I said and found myself laughing at the puzzled look on Frank's face. "Hey, I was raised in Canton, Ohio. Al Capone called it his 'Little Chicago'."

He snuffed out a cigarette, dropping another butt into my cup.

"So how about a local guy named Piazza? He likes to be called 'Butch.' Know about him?"

"No."

"His name is John Piazza. Remember it. How about Mikey Ducks?"

"Nope."

"That's Michael Centoducati, remember that name, too. Sometimes he goes by the street name 'Pie'."

Frank's glance at his wristwatch set him cussing that we were late for our dinner date. He shoved me down the steps, out the door, and hustled me to his big black Buick sedan. He made a show of putting a finger to his lips before unlocking the doors; he motioned for me to hop in the passenger's seat. Once inside, he produced a small device and pressed a button. One light flashed red until its mate blinked green-green-green. I assumed my favorite spook was "sweeping" for hidden recording devices. We spoke not a word until we were well on the freeway heading toward South Miami.

"OK, Morgan, now give me the details of today's fiasco again from start to finish, and if you leave one word out I am going to dump your ass out on Alligator Alley."

I described, in as much detail as I could muster, my daughter's friend sharing the secret that started my day's events. I told him about disguising my car, and myself, detailing everything I saw and did up to and including the explosion.

"Are you positive no one saw you pulling out of there?"

"Yessir."

"Pass any cars?"

"Only that cop that came blowing around the corner, but that was three, four miles down the road."

Once again, we rode in silence until we parked on a dimly lighted backstreet in the heart of Little Havana. He kept me from exiting while he made a production of opening the glove box directly in front of me. It contained an active tape recorder. He pointed that little remote device at it and mashed buttons until it faded to black.

"Lesson Numero Uno to staying alive in Spooksville: when you do something

THE SPOOK TEST

sneaky, wave it right under their noses."

I wasn't sure if I should smile or grimace.

Entering the restaurant in Miami's Little Havana was akin to walking into a 1940s *cinéma noire Casablanca* where Humphrey Bogart and Ingrid Bergman sat huddled at the bar, scheming against the evils of fat-boy Sydney Greenstreet and bug-eyed Peter Lorre.

The mustachioed maître d' greeted Frank effusively and, as we were ushered to a reserved alcove, salutes, winks, and nods came his way from all directions. As was his habit, Frank took the seat with the clearest view of the entrance and then lit the first in a steady chain of cigarettes. I noticed as the evening wore on that they seldom touched his lips; instead, he waved them about his mouth each time he spoke. I would learn this was his way of driving lip readers batty. I took this as my "Lesson Numero Dos" in surviving Spooksville. I wasn't a smoker and didn't want to start, but the rationale drove me to stroke my mustache while uttering secrets.

Frank's customary bottle of capped Coca-Cola and a glass appeared without asking. I noticed early on that he preferred to snap those caps himself, and it had better do a fizz-pop. For myself, I received an extra strong Cuba Libre without asking.

"Look, Beto," Frank muttered, using the street-Spanish nickname he had given me, "I won't argue that any jerk-off who sells drugs to kids shouldn't be pitched into shark water from five thousand feet up, but risking yourself to take down one corner rat is just plain stupid. Know why? Their suppliers can replace them overnight.

"Look, street dealers are junkies themselves; they're not in charge. Go check it out. Next Friday another strung-out idiot will be out there delivering crap to every kid dumb enough to make a buy. Even if you snagged one a week, they'd just send in another."

"OK, so how do I find who is in charge?" I questioned.

Frank rolled his eyes and shook his head. "You came from a mobbed up town, right? So who do you think is running drugs through Florida, Snow White and a bunch of dwarfs?"

"Yeah, but the wiseguys I knew were only about numbers, gambling, prostitution, hijacking, unions, and vending machines. We had zero drugs on the streets except on the dark side of town, and they had their own suppliers. Any jerk-off who'd hustle to any kid would've been chopped up and fed to hogs."

Changing the subject, Frank asked if those Everglades cookers made it out before their shack blew.

"I honestly can't say; I hauled ass out of there. Besides, I could only see one side of that trailer. Maybe they had another door.

"What makes you so sure this is a mobbed up deal?"

He sketched out his theory. The recent increase in addictive drugs hitting America was in direct result to the Soviet Union's embarrassment in the wake of the 1962 Cuban Missile Crisis. Frank called it "Khrushchev's revenge." According to him, and he should know, the Russian KGB had hosted a top-secret meeting in Havana's harbor to arrange a truce between the American Mafia and the Castros. The terms of that truce included the Mafia cancelling its contract to assassinate Fidel and Raul Castro as revenge for confiscating their hotels, casinos, and brothels; in return, the Middle East shipped hard drugs into Cuba where death row inmates would buy more heartbeats by repackaging them. Then, under the cover of night, Cuban government gunboats would transport those packages to prearranged rendezvous points where clusters of Mafia-controlled speedboats hovered barely outside America's territorial limits. At a common signal, all the speedboats would fan out to swarm past the cruising U.S. Coast Guard cutters. It was physically impossible to snag them all.

Upon reaching the assigned contact docks scattered up and down the coast, the drugs were loaded into waiting cars, cans, and trucks. Within hours, untold pounds of heroin and cocaine were en route, ready for nationwide distribution. Thus, Russia reveled in revenge, the Castros were safe, and Meyer Lansky and his pals grew wealthier by the hour through the pain and suffering of American and Canadian junkies young and old.

I was processing this blizzard of information when a burly man with an Irish-red face and a thick New York accent slid onto the seat opposite Frank.

"Hey, how y'doon, Frankie-baby! Had a hell of a time looking around Fort

THE SPOOK TEST

Lauderdale today. Ol' Oscar Fraley's right; it's a good freakin' place to retire." He jerked one thick thumb my way. "Is this the writer guy you tol' me 'bout? How y'doon, kid?"

Wriggling his cigarette around his mouth, Frank said, "Morgan, meet Eddie Egan. He's that Big Apple detective who knocked off that French Connection thing back in '61. What was it, 110 to 120 pounds of pure heroin? Gene Hackman played him in the movie."

"Oh, yeh," I said in my best Brooklynese. "How y'doon, Mr. Egan."

Egan belched a laugh and joined Frank in a stream of ball-busting gibes aimed directly at their newest target. When their good-natured ruckus wound down, Frank brought him up to date about our book and film proposal, but then shocked me by tossing my misadventure into the conversation.

Eddie's grin dissolved, and he said, "With all due respect, Morgan, taking down one, two, or even ten of those punks won't make a dent. You wanna know the only thing that'll hurt 'em? Fahget the street dealers; fahget the 'soldiers,' too. Them bums only take orders from 'made men'; you understand what I'm sayin' here? And even if you got the top dog in Miami and ripped his heart out, the big bosses you'll never see won't care unless it touches their pockets.

"The cancer is always at the top of the organization and never those dumb saps workin' for chump-change. So stick to making movies and keepin' your kid straight. That's the best any civilian can do, know what I mean?"

I slid ten dollars on the table and pushed to my feet.

"Thanks for the advice, Mr. Egan, and for yours too, Frank, but I gotta do what I gotta do. I'll catch a cab north."

Twin pairs of hands slammed me back to my seat and Sturgis snarled into my right ear, "Guess who just got named Miami's most-eligible bachelor among the young, rich, and the ready? John Charles Piazza III, that's who," while Eddie attacked my left ear, "And those dip-shit society reporters have no friggin' clue that he's the son of the don in Atlanta who is in tight with Carlos Marcello. You heard of him, right?"

"Yeah, sure," I said. "Marcello is the New Orleans mobster Bobby Kennedy had snatched and dumped in some Guatemalan jungle. I've heard people swear he was a part of both Kennedy assassinations."

"Damned right he was," Eddie snapped back. "And he's a killer from the get-go. Keep in mind that he and Piazza's old man are still in tight with Joe Bonanno."

"I'd read somewhere he'd retired with a bad heart–to Arizona, I think."

The waiter arrived to serve Eddie a double shot of whiskey, neat, with no chaser. I wondered if he ordered at the bar, or if he was another regular?

"One hundred percent smokescreen," Eddie said when the waiter left. "All that crap about Joe being kidnapped by his cousin, having a heart attack, and then retiring to Arizona is all smoke and mirrors, m'man. Bonanno is the last true *capo di tutti capi*, the 'boss of bosses' to all the American families."

Frank leaned in again. "Remember the guy in the Porsche? He's Butch Piazza's number one enforcer, and he'd eat your liver for breakfast without a burp. And don't ever trust . . ."

Again, we went silent while the waiter served a platter of Cuban-style meat croquettes and shrimp-stuffed avocadoes.

Eddie waited until we were alone before he added, "Piazza's crew is so well organized, the Dade County Strike Force can't even trace his frigging bag-lady to find out who's next in the cash pipeline, and all she uses are public taxicabs to make her drops. Get this; she's lost *every* tail they ever put on her!"

I nearly spit a croquette into his lap when I coughed and gagged. "She uses *what*?"

"Hey, try chewing," Egan smiled.

"Yeah, sure, sorry; she uses what?" I asked again.

"Taxicabs. That broad has been driving everybody nuts with her friggin' act. Anyway, that's the league you're dealing with, so hang up the gloves in that arena and write Frank's story."

"Wait-wait. How can she use a taxicab to disappear? That's impossible!"

Either to humor me or, perhaps, to shut me up, my mentors played tag-team while explaining her act. She would call various companies hours in advance to pre-schedule a daisy chain of cabs from different companies, each destined to rendezvous at timed intervals but at widely scattered points. For instance,

THE SPOOK TEST

cab number one would pick her up at the David William Residence Hotel in Coral Gables and she would instruct that driver to drive her to some common destination such as a mall or a movie theater. En route, she would complain about some phantom boyfriend who might follow her, so she would order him to use backstreets while she watched for undercover police cars or even helicopters. A legitimate cabbie–they had tried using undercover cops as drivers with no success–could care less because he is paid by the minute.

However, before they could reach her original destination, she would change her mind and order him to take a screwball route–turn here, turn-there–to where she had scheduled a second taxi. The first car barely halted before she would flip a wad of loose bills his way and leap into the next cab.

She would continue cab swapping until she was certain the cops had given up, and then she would vanish.

Frank and Eddie sat gaping when I commenced rocking back-and-forth, giggling. How could they know that my new storyline for Quinn Martin involved a taxi driver who solved crimes for the frustrated Miami Police Department? What better material could I ask for than a real gig? Maybe, *just maybe* I might track that clever bag lady all the way to her secret destination.

Of course, I had no idea how–or if–I might pull this off, but somehow lyrics from the song, *With a Little Help from My Friends*, came to mind, so I shared my new storyline with my dinner partners.

"Are you nuts?" Frank barked through a cloud of blue smoke. "They'd whack you in a heartbeat!"

"Jesus freakin' Keerist," Eddie chimed in. "This ain't no movie, pal. This is real life!"

This time I was happy when our waiter commenced serving an unbroken stream of Caribbean delicacies. In between courses, they chastised, berated, warned, and lectured until finally accepting that I was determined to become the "bag lady's" next taxi driver.

They spent the remainder of our evening putting me through a cram course of the "do-this-and-never-do-that" routines. Better yet, Frank agreed to score a job for me at South Miami's Turtle Taxicab Company under a fictitious name, a favor he could manage because the manager and the night dispatcher were Cuban refugees who owed him favors. The yarn he would use was that my "ex-wife" had become a call girl and the fare I sought was the madam who could lead me to her.

Frank made but one demand: I must remove his telephone numbers from my wallet.

Today's readers might not know much about John Charles Piazza III. In 1976, Dade County, Florida, federal drug agents knew that Piazza operated a large-scale drug operation in the Southeast. In 1977, one of Piazza's narcotics couriers agreed to cooperate with federal authorities, including the DEA, the Bureau of Alcohol, Tobacco, Firearms and Explosives (ATF), and Organized Crime Strike Force, investigating the Piazza case due to an arrest for narcotics trafficking and homicide. The courier, William Zambito, was protected from other imprisoned co-defendants, including Centoducati ("Mikey Ducks"). Within a year of being imprisoned and waiting to help the government to solidify their case, Zambito was fatally stabbed while in prison.

Later, after Piazza was arrested and linked to more than twenty homicides, he agreed to cooperate with federal authorities and became what many dubbed a "professional witness" against the mob. He testified in varied cases, including against Anthony "Tumac" Accetturo, a reputed Mafia associate with the Lucchese organized crime family in New York.

Piazza's family reportedly was brought into the Trafficante crime family as early as the 1940s. After Santo Trafficante Sr. died in 1954, he passed the reigns to his son, Santo Trafficante Jr. The core of the Trafficante family operates out of Tampa and Miami. It is the only crime family organized in Florida.

3 TAXI!

The dispatcher at Turtle Taxicab Company on South Dixie Highway shouted in a strong Spanish accent "Aieee! Si, si! I know that puta! She always say to get her a driver quick or I should go to fucking hell! *Muy loco*, her!"

He went on to rant that the mystery woman called about twice a month on random days, but always in the evening. She would demand that he deliver a cab within five minutes of her call. If the cabbie was late, she vanished, but she always called him back the following day to raise holy hell. He went on to say he would do this favor for Frank but, after that, he would never send her another cab. I calmed him down by promising him every dime earned from every other fare if he would just arrange for me to be hovering near her hotel each and every evening.

"OK, man, jus' don't keel that beetch in my cab."

I knew that, in reality, I had a slim-to-none chance to transport this professional "bag lady" to her final destination. From what I understood, she had been outsmarting professional task forces for months, but I had to try, didn't I?

By day, I began drafting Frank's book and film proposals. By night, I was just another cabbie wearing a scrunched-down old Navy watch cap and a raunchy attitude.

In truth, I expected driving a cab would be a series of boring trips to and from the airport or carting grannies to supermarkets and shopping malls. Indeed, I had my share of such chores, yet I was astonished at what nonsense cabbies sometimes endure to make a buck.

For instance, I was less than a week into my charade when a hysterical woman threatened to bail out at 65 miles per hour on a crowded freeway because she'd just caught her husband in bed with her mother. I reacted by yelling that if she took that leap I would lose my job, go to jail, and my six kids would starve. I wailed that she'd burn forever in Hell and she'd never ever see Jesus.

I made such a show that she didn't notice when I whipped the taxi off at the next exit, searching for the first church I could find. Fate was kind; I found one still open and hustled her out of my cab, through the doors, and down the aisle as fast as her legs would wobble. That old adage about being left at the altar took on a new meaning because the moment her knees hit the carpet, I beat-feet for the nearest exit.

However, my scariest fare came near the end of a Saturday night shift when I responded to a call in the upscale suburban neighborhood of Kendall Lakes, southwest of Miami. I had barely paused at the address when a burly man with a sweaty face and hairy hands leaped into my rear seat clad only in silk pajamas and flip-flops. Speaking in a thick Jersey accent, he roared that his wife had locked him out because he had slapped her around.

"Can you believe that bitch? She was nuttin' but a freakin' tramp when I picked her outta the gutter and I made her into freakin' lady."

"Err, where to, sir?"

"Move, move! Get me to the nearest freakin' phone–holy *shit!*"

An entire line of police cars appeared dead ahead, roaring straight at us with sirens blaring and lights flashing.

"She freakin' did it! Don't stop, don't stop; get me outta here! Go, go!" my passenger yelled, squeezing his bulk down behind my seat. At first, I floored it straight toward the cop cars, and then I slowed to a crawl.

"You rat-fink mutha! I'll sink you inna bay; I'll drop you inna ocean and chum for sharks! You're a freakin' dead man!" my fare wailed.

I slowly-slowly turned right onto a quiet residential side street and cruised along as if searching for an address while the cop cars whizzed by.

My passenger popped up as the sirens faded.

"Good thinking,' kid! I could use a smart driver. Want a job?"

TAXI!

"Thanks, but I'm moving back to Cleveland. Where to?"

"Get me to a phone; you know, one of those outside ones. Got a quarter?"

I knew of a convenience store along the Dixie Highway that had an outside phone booth. However, I made the mistake of shutting off the cab's engine and lowering the windows to get a whiff of the night air. How could I help but hear him ordering "Joey" to rent a suite in his name at a Coral Gables hotel on Le Jeune Road and order a bottle of Chavez Regal.

"Now lissen up," he growled into the phone's receiver, "and I ain't changing my mind this time. I want that bitch dead before dawn, understand? Don't argue; just give me time to check in so I can make myself a pain in the ass by calling the desk all freakin' night. Be sure to snatch her jewelry–take the big stuff so I can claim it–and put jimmy marks on the back door like it was busted into. How? Use the freaking key I gave you! Oh, and be sure to dial 'zero' on the phone and put it in her hand before you bust that big clock in the hall. Why? So's the time on the phone call matches the clock, you moron!"

His final order to Joey was to have clothes, underwear, shoes, and socks delivered at the hotel before 10 a.m.

I had collapsed over the steering wheel and didn't move when he thumped back inside. He shook my shoulder. "Hey, you OK? What's a matter with you?"

"W-what? Oh, wow, I'm sorry, sir, I zonked out," I yawned. "I've been working double shifts for a month. Please don't tell my boss, please? I need the bread. Where to?"

"I already told you. Let's go!"

You are a liar, I thought, but I said, "I guess I forgot. I get nervous when I see cop cars, know what I mean?"

"Yeah, OK, so just head north on Dixie."

We drove in silence until we approached Coral Gables.

"Take a left on Le Jeune Road. You keep a log, right?"

"Yessir."

"Make sure you put me down at the right time, got it?"

"Yessir, and the dispatcher logs it when I call to tell him where I am."

"What's the fare?"

"Eight-twenty, sir."

"You gotta eat it tonight but it'll be made good."

He waited, listening while I called in before he marched into that fancy lobby in his silk pajamas.

When I reported to work the following evening, I received an envelope containing the exact fare, a fifty-dollar tip, plus a shiny new quarter for the telephone.

I refused to read a newspaper for a month.

Time had about run out on my scheme to find the "Bag Lady." My current film was due for its premiere screening the following weekend and it was a given that I would be appearing in the media. However, my last few days as a nameless cabbie were proving unusually busy and my dispatcher's patience was running out. He called once, twice, three times to order-ask-plead that I help him out by taking fares. I felt horrible, but refused.

Then it happened. Excited, he ordered me to the David William Residence Hotel *muy pronto*. My target was awaiting pickup.

Tires squealing, I barely nosed out a Yellow Cab to make it first in line before the polished doors of the hotel. To my dismay, out marched a pursed-mouthed, elderly dowager sporting a 1930s-style pillbox hat complete with a veil, a Carol Lombard-style suit with squared-off shoulders, and lace gloves. Close behind her loped a tall and slender nymph with a bulging handbag she clutched with both hands. Feeling and acting the cad, I body-blocked the sputtering older woman, ushering the younger beauty into my cab's rear seat.

Hollywood had it wrong when they portrayed bag ladies as haggy old broads one step away from skid row. This one was in her mid-twenties, long-limbed, sloe-eyed, olive-skinned, with teeth that were small but perfect, nipping the ends off every word.

"Kendall Mall," she snipped. "Take Coral Way to the Palmetto Expressway, use only the right lane, and stay under the speed limit," she commanded while her head swiveled right, left and back again to complete a 360-degree sweep.

"Er, beautiful evening, isn't it?" I offered with my Sunday smile. "Got enough cool air back there?"

TAXI!

She checked to make sure my cabbie ID fit my face, then returned to scanning.

"Did you catch Jack Nicholson in *One Flew Over the Cuckoo's Nest*," I asked. "I worked at a mental hospital once as a kid. I knew that Nurse Ratched's twin, if you know what I mean. Hell, I identified more with patients than any of the staff ... funny, huh?"

"I've changed my mind; go south on Grenada," she commanded. "Turn here, damn it, and then take me back through the Gables; use Almeria until I tell you different," she said, continuing to turn her head like a human radar dish.

"Excuse me, miss; you got a problem? Maybe I can help."

"I'm paying you to drive, not talk–and I told you not to speed," she said icily.

"Speed limit's twenty-five; I'm doing fifteen."

She checked my cabbie ID again.

"Is Morgan your real name?"

"It's actually Einstein, but no one would believe me."

"I'm writing it down."

"E-i-n-s-t-e-i-n. Want my phone number, too?"

"That'll be the day, smart ass," she mocked.

"Hey, I gotta call in to dispatch so they don't schedule me fares out of Kendall. Where are we headed?" I asked as I queued up dispatch.

"Tell them I'm a tourist and want to see some sights."

I did.

"Si, senorrrrr, yo comprendo," the dispatcher smirked back. I switched him off.

"OK, so now where, ma'am?"

"Downtown Miami, Flagler and Biscayne. Take the Dixie Highway, stay in the right lane and five miles under the speed limit."

"That's a long way from Kendall Mall ..."

"It's my dime, asshole. Get over in the right lane."

Did I hear that right? Did this gangster's bitch in pretty skin, the one carrying a bag stuffed full of drug money raked in from kids and lost dope-heads, did she just call me . . .? Maybe I should pitch her out on her pretty tush out and swipe her stash of cash? What could she do, call the cops? Better yet, she could send her mob-boys after me and I would arrange a meet-and-greet with one of Frank's anti-Castro Cuban crews. I'd be glad to donate her entire stash to their cause. I pacified myself with a rant.

We were fast approaching the entrance to Miami's Science Museum when she leaned forward to hiss in my ear, "You aren't fooling me, jerk-off. I know my rights and I demand that you pull over right now and let me out."

"Hey, lady, you said Flagler and Biscayne . . . "

"Don't give me that innocent bullshit. Unless you produce a warrant and read me my rights, it's unlawful restraint and kidnapping if you don't pull over when I tell you to. Let me out and maybe I won't sue you and your department jointly and severally. Got that? *There, there!* Pull over!"

Just as Frank and Eddie had predicted, there was another cab waiting to begin her game of tag.

Screw it. Snatching off my watch cap and mashing the gas pedal to the floor, I swerved into the speed lane.

"Son of a bitch, kid," I yelled at her. "Who gave me up? Damn it, damn, it, *damn it!"*

"There's the museum; stop, stop, stop! I'll sue!" she screeched while pawing at the door handle. No worries. She wasn't going to bail out at 50 to 60 miles per hour in that traffic and chance spilling all that money, not to mention being pulverized in traffic.

"You know who I am, don't you?" I shouted back. "Aw, *mannnnnn,* tell me what shmuck gave me up and maybe you'll live to see tomorrow."

"Pull over, goddamn you! Do it, do it, do it!"

"Tell me who gave me up, you sneaky bitch," I snarled as we barreled up the ramp to burst onto the busy U.S. 1 six-lane freeway. "If it's that freaking dispatcher, I'll have his Cuban ass on a plate. That son of a BITCH."

"You're really a cop, aren't you?" squeaked my rapidly melting Ice Lady.

"Yeah, sure, I'm Sam Spade, private eye. So who are you with, Ivan Tors Studios? Are they sniffing around again? Oh, I get it. You're out of LA. Can't

TAXI!

anyone out there ever deal from the top of the deck?"

"You have to let me out," she stuttered. "I-I-I know my rights!"

"Bat crap! You've got no rights now that you're riding on *my* dime. I'm out here busting my ass trying to get good stories and you pull this crap on me? To hell with you and whoever your boss is! I'll take my project to another network! I've registered everything with the Writers Guild, you got that?"

I nearly burst out laughing when I turned to glare at her. The one-time toughie was close to epileptic shock.

"Please, please let me out," she whined. "I swear to God . . . I'm only doing what I'm told!"

"Aw, chill out, kid. It's not your fault," I said. "I know you're only doing your job. So which studio is it?"

"I don't know anything about studios."

"As beautiful as you are? Come on. A reporter, then? Look, give me a break or maybe I'll have to toss your pretty butt into the bay as shark bait. See, if you print any of this, everybody in town will know what I'm working on and they'll steal it. I've already lost one good TV series and a feature to the crooked head of the Ivan Tors Studios because I was a trusting idiot. Come on, kid, you look like a nice person–are you an actress? Maybe I could work you in."

"Wait, look! There's Flagler Street! Please, I have another cab I need to catch and I won't turn you in, I swear!"

"Turn me in? Kid, you've got me all messed up," I said, staying in the fast lane. "I'll tell you what; I'll take you anywhere you want to go if you'll promise not to print any of this crap. I have a film due for release and you could ruin it for me, OK? It's the first one that I wrote, directed, and co-produced, and our investors want to roll over. It's the break of a lifetime, so don't mess me up, alright?"

"I really, really, really don't know what you're talking about," she whined. I felt her warm breath on my neck.

I handed her a business card that she read several times before asking why I was driving a taxi. I swore her to secrecy before telling her my concept of that Cuban ex-cop solving crimes.

"Oh God, that's huge; that's fabulous," she gushed.

CITIZEN SPY

I noted, too, that we were still rolling north toward Fort Lauderdale and she was not correcting me so I rattled on about having been featured in The Smithsonian TV series, *Monsters: Myth or Mystery*, and having had the lead in Bostonia Film Productions' feature-length docudrama, *The Search for Bigfoot*, blah, blah, blah. And yes, I shamelessly dropped actors' names with whom I had worked: William Shatner, Ruth Roman, Jennifer Bishop, Harold "Oddjob" Sakata of *Goldfinger* fame, John Chandler, Kenny Miller, and more. I bragged, too, that a few of my concepts had evolved into the feature films *Jaws of Death* and *Lucky Lady* with Burt Reynolds, Liza Minnelli, and Gene Hackman.

As I yakked on, my alter ego as the secret son of Humphrey Bogart's Sam Spade, private eye, deduced that because she was not correcting our route we must be heading toward her true destination. I hid my sly grin while my fare lady cooed on that she was a huge fan of James Bond films and would I pretty-please introduce her to Oddjob should he ever come to town? Also, would I . . .

"Wait! Slow down, turn, turn," she screeched. I dodged over through three lanes of horn-blowing traffic, peeling off at the 125th Street exit. From there she directed me east to the new and plush Big Daddy's nightclub perched at the edge of the Intercoastal Waterway, just shy of Bal Harbour.

The greeter opened her door. "Olga! Hey, you're way early!"

To me, she said, "I'm going to check out everything you said, and by the way, I think you are *so* cute. I'm keeping your card, too!"

"Please do," I said as the attendant flipped me a pair of twenty-dollar bills to cover a thirty-seven dollar fare.

Fine. Jolly-good, mate. I didn't care. Maybe the Dade County Strike Force's finest sleuths didn't know where this bag lady delivered her loot, but suddenly I did, didn't I!

4 — MY FARE LADY

The following morning, my happy drive to the office was crammed with nefarious plots, plans, and schemes to wreak revenge upon my doubters. First, I would (ahem!) humbly announce to Frank and Eddie that I had quit hacking for Turtle Cab. I would, of course, weather their congratulations for coming to my senses. Then, when the guffaws had run their course, I would reveal that mysterious bag lady's true name is Olga, tell them that she delivers the mob's loot to the Big Daddy's nightclub outside Bal Harbour, that the doorman there is cheap, and furthermore (*snort-snort*) that the bag lady the Dade County Task Force can't follow thinks I'm *cute*!

I was singing along with Jimmy Buffet's newest hit *Margaritaville* when I wheeled into the parking area adjacent to Creative Film & Sound. It was too early for our lovely Nina to be in the office, but I . . . my heart stopped.

My throat went dry as a desert ditch in July. Last night's bag lady was pacing back and forth in front of our front door, like a cat on a short leash; her puffy eyes and messy hair screamed that she was not a happy camper. Not yet spotting me, she shrugged her shoulders in the general direction of a large sedan parked directly across the street. Therein a thick figure hunched behind the wheel of a too-new, too-clean, and too-polished Lincoln Continental; the driver's face was masked nose-down by an open newspaper and brows-up by a dark ball cap.

Frank's advice returned like a mantra. "*Lesson Numero Uno to staying alive *in Spooksville; when you do something sneaky, wave it under their noses . . . when you do something sneaky, wave it under their noses . . . when you do something sneaky . . ."*

I smothered the urge to shout at that mug in the Lincoln those immortal words of tough-guy actor Edward G. Robinson, "Come and get me, you dirty rat. I'm Rico, Junior; I'm Little Caesar's grandkid, *nyahhhhh!*" I didn't, though. This was no movie, these were no actors, and damned few guns around Miami fired blanks. Instead, I rushed over to give last night's fare a happy hug and lots of air-kisses.

Chattering like a monkey on the make, I ushered Olga inside and gave her the grand tour of our sound stage. She stared at the 16mm Arriflex cameras perched atop tripods like hawks waiting for their next meal; she inspected the props, microphones, and snaky cables that crisscrossed the floor. She gaped at the recording booth with its banks of knobs, dials, switches, and sliders all left messy amid Stan Webb's overflowing ashtrays and crushed beer cans.

To balance the picture, I allowed her a peek inside Mitzi's squeaky-clean cutting room where dozens of film clips dangled from nylon lines and white gloves were the order of the day.

Lastly, I admitted her to the second-floor inner sanctum office that Irv Rudley and I shared, where she took inventory of our gallery of celebrity photos. Of course, she made all the usual gurgles about their inscriptions, but that wise child also swiped a finger over the top of their frames to ensure they were not new props.

Satisfied with the dust, she whirled about to announce that we must, must, *must* celebrate last night's meeting by sharing a *fabulous* champagne brunch at the fashionable Doubletree Hotel in Coconut Grove; her treat, of course. Could I pretty-please get away, as in immediately because she was simply *famished?*

"Oh, and may I use your rest room," she giggled. "I saw it as we came in so you don't need to show me. My ride was in a convertible and I must look like Raggedy Ann," she fibbed as she snatched a comb from her bag and clumped down the stairs.

Liar, liar, pants on fire, I thought.

MY FARE LADY

I fought a powerful urge to tiptoe down behind her so I could sneak out through the studio's back door. Suddenly, I heard a faint, very faint noise. *Listen-listen!* My ears strained to hear. The front door squeaked open, paused, and then squeaked closed again. Was she ushering in that mystery huncher from across the street? Oh, how I wished my Maggie May was in my pocket instead of in my car. Wait, why had my ultra-secretive visitor taken only her comb and left her tote bag with its mouth gaping?

Unable to resist, I peeked inside. Indeed, there was a live tape recorder in action.

I tossed Frank a mental thank you for his lesson and reverted to Morgan's Maxim: when in doubt, attack!

Solely for her benefit, I planted an Easter Egg on her recorder by faking a telephone call to the McDermott Agency and went through the expected hellos before loudly bragging that my research project about taxi driving was completed and, "yes, yes," I also would have a draft proposal ready for Quinn Martin within the week. Yes, too, best-selling author Oscar Fraley was on board to help with the book and I was proposing a pilot film about Frank Sturgis and his escapades with Castro and CIA. Indeed, my contract with Frank and Fraley was already inked. Hearing Olga ascending the steps, I made bye-bye noises as she entered the office with a grin fit for a Colgate ad.

"Shall we go?" she bubbled.

"Um, maybe I'd better beg off. I have a hell of a lot of work to do. Give me a number and I'll call."

"But I just sent my ride away!"

"Hey, I have an in with a cab company, remember?"

"What did I do? How did I insult you, Morgan?"

"M'love, my momma always said that I must never do brunch, lunch, dinner, or supper with a beautiful lady unless I at least know her name."

"You are a real brat! I'm Olga."

"Olga from the Volga or . . .?"

"Half of my name is worth half of your day. If we are still talking after half of the day, then maybe then I will fill in the blank. Oh, and would you be a darling and allow me to make a private call? I'm expecting something important so I have to stay in contact with my service."

I bounded downstairs and made a beeline for the front door. The Continental had vanished. I watched the buttons on our switchboard. The upstairs line was busy for a fraction of a minute. I waited in silence, knowing she was reviewing her tape. One minute, two minutes, three minutes, four. Olga descended the steps on cue.

We kept our banter light and breezy over brunch. Apparently, I was saying things that intrigued her because our day extended into a stroll through every over-priced jewelry, clothing, and art gallery in sight. I extracted my revenge for wasting my heartbeats pouring over gewgaw by talking ad nauseum about how we had to scrounge for investors for my script *Let's Kill Charlie Angel* that I had created for Harold Sakata, Sam Melville of *The Rookies*, Jennifer Bishop of every man's dream, and my all-time favorite bad-guy, John Davis Chandler.

It was somewhat irksome that instead of being bored she became increasingly attentive, especially when I dipped into the fine points of how enormous profits were possible for independent films, but only if one hooked up with the right distributor. I explained the key was to keep another marketable film loaded into the breech as a follow-up. The hungrier the distributors were for your next product, the more likely they were to pay at least a portion of what they actually owed without having to apply a brickbat to their accountant.

Interestingly, the more detailed I became, the more often she stopped at public telephones. Her excuse was she must check in frequently with her service, yet she always returned with a fresh list of apropos questions. Was she being coached what to ask next? By whom? And why?

That first day melded into the evening to conclude at Monty's Conch, an open-air bistro on Bayshore Drive. Bored until now, I perked up when I saw a poster announcing my favorite folksinger and close friend Teri DeSario was the lead act. Upon spotting us, Teri flashed me a grin, a wink, and a nod. All too obviously, she set about teasing me with her sexiest song, *It's So Good to be With You*. Olga's olive skin quickly became a ticked-off bronze. Obviously, she was accustomed to being the top bill no matter how fresh the relationship.

MY FARE LADY

Unfortunately for Olga, she lost out on my attentions when Teri was around.

Evening over, I dropped her off at the David William, the same spot where we had met the previous evening. As I held the door, she whispered that her full name was Olga Elias, and then she kissed me.

My, my, I thought as I drove away. Pull the thread, get a string; pull the string, get a rope; pull the rope and perhaps you might get a noose to hang a dope dealer?

Too happy to cave in and go home, I zipped back to Monty's to catch Teri's closing act.

The telephone was ringing when I walked into my office the following morning.

"Morgan, you are such a stinker! Why didn't you tell me you knew Frank Sturgis? Could you please, please introduce my very, very, *very* important friend to him? He needs some insider advice about Cuba, and he'll make it worth your while, honest! And by the way, he also wants to talk with you about his own story; you know, like what you're doing with Mr. Sturgis. Guess what else? He wants to know how he might get involved in financing your films."

My mind stopped spinning at three bars–*jackpot!* Obviously, she had reviewed her sneaky recording and swallowed my speech hook, line, and sinker.

"And who is this mystery man, dear Olga?"

"I can't tell you that just yet, dear Morgan! He'll do that in his own time. He's the private sort, you know."

I made nice-nice sounds and promised to forward her request to Frank as I was meeting him within the hour. When I did, he nearly spat coffee in my lap.

"You want me to do what? I'm fresh out of prison and you want me to meet some mob bag lady and her boss? I have three answers for you, Morgan. No, no, and *hell* no."

"OK, OK; I just thought . . ."

"No, you didn't think! Look, let's just pass along what you've learned to the task force and forget about it. They'll wait a while and then take her down when she meets up with whomever at Big Daddy's. Trust me, those idiots will squeal like pigs rather than face jail time. You'll have done your duty as a good father and we can get back to business."

"Frank, she also wants to introduce me to someone who can finance my films, so that's not some loose-change schmuck. It's gotta be Piazza or maybe one of the bigger boys."

"Give it up, Morgan," Sturgis groaned.

"Hey, this is her idea, not mine. I need to know what makes them tick and then I guarantee you I'll turn everything over to whomever you say."

"You're absolutely certain you want to go through with this?" Frank questioned.

At my nod, he launched to his feet.

"OK, lover-boy, let's get your education started. I have an appointment for lunch at the Diplomat where you can stick your toe in the water. Don't get sweaty palms, cheapskate. It'll be my buy this time."

My palms got sweaty anyway. I knew he played in the big leagues and the Diplomat Hotel in Hallandale was a legendary haunt of the wise-guy elite.

Our trip north became a nonstop lecture about Mafia structure, protocols, pet peeves, and pitfalls. Henceforth, he told me that I must cooperate with Olga and permit her the final say about where and when we should meet, but I must not bitch when she changes plans mid-stream; that's part of their game of self-protection. However, from time-to-time, I must refuse minor requests. A 100 percent kiss-ass loses respect.

In addition, allow Olga random access to my briefcase, office files, and Rolodex, but only *after* I sanitize them of family photographs, true telephone numbers and addresses. Meet any query about the whereabouts of my daughter with comments that the subject is too painful to discuss. Indeed, because my ex-wife's family was Canadian, let it slip they both are returning there permanently.

Other Sturgis rules of engagement required that I appear single-minded about my professional projects, and I must especially ignore everything I might overhear Olga say either in my presence or within earshot. Most likely, this type of gem was nothing more than bait for traps. Equally as important, if left alone in her private space, I must assume that either I am under surveillance or there are tiny traps to indicate tampering. This rule especially applied if ledgers, letters, files, or notes are left in plain sight or easily accessible. In short, I should appear supremely single-minded in my acts yet acutely aware of everything.

He also warned that from time-to-time, I would be overpaid. I must be honest about thousands of dollars but never the hundreds. Scrupulous honesty smells like a cop. In addition, if asked to perform personal favors, I must consider them orders. Moreover, if questioned, I must assume they know the answers.

Lastly, whenever I needed to talk with Frank about my mission, we must meet in person or use public telephones. Even then, it would be wise if I spoke using one hand cupped around my mouth except when talking about other things.

My mind was reeling by this point. All that said, he provided me a list of his personal contact numbers at differing locations. They were in numerical order of one through six. I must encode these numbers within my pocket telephone book but scattered amid legitimate contacts. For example, I must select the third to last name on pages that began with the alternate letters B, D, F, H, J, and L. His private numbers must appear beneath the true number assigned to that person. However, the middle two digits of the last four numbers must be reversed. I looked baffled so he gave me an example. In example, the number 555-9915 would appear as 555-9_19_5.

To signal me to call him at a specific number, he would drop a comment about something on page three of our book proposal, script, or the daily newspaper. I would then return his call using his phone number under the encrypted letter "F." As additional protection, he suggested that I apply the same coding to my family numbers.

Upon arrival at the posh Diplomat Hotel, Frank made a point of parking in the least-crowded section of the lot. He explained that clusters of cars provide cover for unwanted encounters. His final words of advice were that I must not believe a word he says that afternoon until we were back in the car. Even then, I should not speak until he checked his sound-activated recorder to ensure there had been no intruder who might have placed a bug.

CITIZEN SPY

I hummed Shirley Bassey's rendition to the Oscar-winning film *Goldfinger* all the way to the hotel's dining room until being struck speechless when the nattily dressed maître d' stepped forward to greet us each by name. Ernest G. Sloan and I took turns explaining to Frank that the previous week, Fraley had introduced us to discuss the film potential of Sloan's novel, *Behind the Velvet Rope*. At that introductory meeting, Ernie had no reason to mention his position at The Diplomat.

However, it was Ernie's turn to sputter when he learned that Frank and I intended to lunch together. As he scuttled off, he said something about our table not being ready and could we *please* be patient a few moments.

"They expected me to come alone," Frank said, chuckling.

"I can wait at the bar."

"No, no, but remember that mobsters never share personal space with people they don't know. We'll probably be put on ice until they look you over. By this time next week, they'll know what you had for supper a month ago."

A few minutes later Ernie escorted us through the crowded dining room to a semi-private one. Only one table was occupied, yet we were ushered to another across the room. En route, Frank exchanged nods with three swarthy men who were picking through platters of hors d'oeuvres. The fourth seat at their table was vacant yet fully set. In seconds, a waiter arrived with Frank's customary soft drink plus a bottle of Syrah wine from the Sicilian Planeta vineyard for me. The men at the opposite table lifted their glasses in *salut*. I felt a chill; I recognized one as the notorious don Santo Trafficante, Jr.

Frank's fist smacked our table.

"I can't believe Ernie let a damned bug in here," he growled, kicking my ankle. "But let's not tell him; he'd take it personally."

I hid my grin. In our proposal, *Lies Our Fathers Told Us*, he described pulling that same bug-warning act in Havana when he was Castro's inspector for Mafia-owned casinos. He was meeting with Johnny Roselli and that was his way of letting that gangster know he knew he was recording their conversation. Now he was signaling me that our wait in the foyer transpired simply to allow a microphone to be taped into place. A quick finger twist against his lips ordered

MY FARE LADY

me to be silent.

"As I was saying, Morgan, we should stick a lot of that Castro crap into our book and screenplay," he said. He went on to describe an argument he had with Castro when he'd ordered all the casinos in Havana shuttered while turning over the most elegant of Havana's hotels to the dumbest of the dumb. While Frank cared about folks in trouble, he complained those ignorant slobs had set about smashing everything in sight. Frank wistfully opined that Cuba had been better off when certain American business interests were attracting buckets of money from around the world to its hotels, casinos, restaurants, tourist traps and, of course, its whorehouses. Of course, the unsaid was that the "American business interests" were, in fact, the American Mafia.

Dinners enjoyed, napkins folded, and check comp'd by an unknown wallet, Frank excused himself to perform the obligatory *abrazos* with Trafficante and his guests and accepted their empty seat. I sat alone feeling like an unwanted stepchild until Santo himself waved me over.

"Aye, Roberto, I hear you wanna make a movie about our Frankie-boy, eh?" he rasped. "*Buono! Fantastico!* Me, I should play myself, but you gotta let me say my lines my way so I can keep his bullshit straight. Whaddya think?"

Although he was kidding, my commercial side drooled at the thought of having a true-life don in front of my cameras. Nevertheless, and in keeping with the mood, I replied that Frank had warned me that portraying his love life might require a wide-angle lens. When the howls ebbed, I added that his girlfriends had whispered that I'd better shoot his action with them in slow motion because it lasted less than a minute.

Amid the second round of choking gasps, Don Santo croaked, "If Frankie drove you up from Miami you'd better call a friggin' cab!"

Ball busting over, maître d'hôtel par excellence Ernie Sloan appeared on cue to usher me to the lounge. He advised that whatever I wished was on the house, adding that to celebrate our friendship, his wife Anne must soon create for us a sumptuous dinner drawn from her Sicilian heritage.

I watched him hustle away with the bearing of a man proud of his profession.

CITIZEN SPY

Born to a reasonably affluent Jewish family in Berlin, Germany, early in life he began his apprenticeship to become a waiter at the finest of restaurants. Unlike rough-hewn America, this profession required years of training in the proper setting of a table, the timing between services, and being conversant with the preparations of the most delicate and exotic of dishes. Being a waiter to the elite classes of Europe was more than a job; it was a profession.

Alas, with Adolf Hitler's rise to power, the Sloans joined the crowds of Jews desperately fleeing Germany to escape the Nazi concentration camps. By chance, they discovered an Italian shipping line that provided passage to Shanghai, China, where no visa was required. Indeed, that bustling port city quickly became a melting pot for refugee Jews, Russians, and American draft dodgers.

However, while Shanghai was the Sloan's haven from the Nazis, it also became a target for invasion of all China by the imperialist Japanese.

A bright lad who knew how to turn a buck, Ernie discovered that smuggling arms to the Chinese underground was more satisfying than waiting tables to bandy-legged Japs. Unfortunately, under the orders of General Eiichi Kino-shita, Ernie and his father were arrested, beaten, and starved in the dreaded Bridge House Prison. Judged uncooperative, the sadistic Sergeant Bunzo Yoshida interrogated the Sloans. Ernie's father died from his beatings and starvation and Ernie was delirious by the time the United States dropped its atomic bombs on Hiroshima and Nagasaki. Scant days later, he was set free.

Ernie managed to return his mother to her native Germany before booking his own passage to America. He was determined to make a success of his life as the ultimate maître d'hôtel. It was inevitable that he became the darling of the American Mafia elite, who appreciated both his Old World manners and his *chutzpah*.

Indeed, Ernie Sloan had outrageous stories to tell, and that's where I came in.

I was nursing my fifth martini when Frank came, crooking a finger for me to follow him. We were silent until he checked the recorder in his car. All was kosher, so we headed home. We discussed many things along the way, but he spoke not a word about what had occurred between him and Trafficante's group.

MY FARE LADY

At Frank's insistence, I advised Olga that because he was a paroled felon, it was not in her best interest to meet Sturgis face-to-face. Instead, he had appointed me their go-between.

That seemed to satisfy her, but she insisted that I introduce her to friends I had claimed among the local Native Americans. Frank's opinion was that someone in their *cosca,* or Sicilian "clan," may have heard me describing my Everglades adventures to then-WKAT radio talk show hosts Larry King or Bill Smith and were testing my veracity. From a mobster's perspective, it would be inconceivable that anyone would hang out with the Native American Miccosukee or Seminole tribesmen just for the hell of it.

They could not have been more wrong; it was among those *true* human beings that I felt most comfortable.

At our first opportunity, I led Olga, my Coral Gables clotheshorse, out to squat beside an evening campfire deep in the Everglades. Donna Tiger, a teenage Miccosukee, handed Olga a chunk of freshly roasted fish while her younger brother, Spencer, popped the tab of a soda can for her.

She took a tiny nibble.

"This isn't bass; I know bass," she said.

"That's gar," Donna replied, sucking her fingers one-by-one.

Olga stared at the charred carcass lying on a tin cookie platter.

"My God, it's huge," she said.

"Aw, this one's just a baby," Donna shrugged. "Grown up they could get as long as six to eight feet if those city boys would just let 'em alone. We don't like those guys. They catch our gar and then leave 'em on the banks to rot. They call it sport; we call it stupid."

Olga took another nibble. "This is really good."

"We always do 'em in campfires," Spencer said.

"You mean over it?" Olga pressed.

"*In* it," Spencer clarified.

"Oh, really? So what do you put on it, lemons and spices?"

"Just the fire and then our lips," he giggled.

Robert, the eldest Tiger, arrived, scraping his canoe onto the bank, and delivering a much bigger gar. When he tossed it onto the hot coals, it flipped and flopped back out. He smacked it with a rock and booted it back in.

"Oh-my-*god*," yelped Olga. "It was still *alive!*"

"Nah," Spencer said. "It just thinks it is."

"But it's whole–don't you clean them first?"

"Can't clean gar, ma'am," Robert said in his solemn way. "Scales are too tough. So, we whack 'em on the head and kick 'em in the fire. They're ready to eat when the scales burn off and the juice stops oozing."

"Dumb-ass city people call 'em trash fish," Spencer snorted. "But our gar's the only fish out here that ain't got worms. I don't eat bass. They got more worms than you can count, but gar are always so clean you could eat 'em raw."

Donna cocked her head at the sound of a bullfrog's croak somewhere close by.

"Miss Olga, do you want to try some frog legs? Won't take but a minute to gig some. C'mon, I'll show you how."

Olga did a quick glance at her wristwatch.

"Oh, thanks, I'd really love to, but just look at the time; I still have a bunch of phone calls to make. Bobby, do you mind if we go now? I really have to hurry."

The Tiger kids hid their grins and accepted my winks, allowing Olga and I to retreat gracefully. Olga spent the entire drive back meticulously picking leaves and lint from her usually pristine clothing.

Safe again in her air-conditioned glass-and-steel suite, she whipped up a pitcher of vodka martinis, poured twin drinks for each of us, gulped hers, and then rushed away to take a quick shower. When she returned all freshly scrubbed and oiled, she insisted that I sit in one particular spot of her couch where she curled up at my feet as if to anchor me in place; undoubtedly, her sneaky tape recorder close by.

"OK, Bobby, please tell me what you and Sturgis are planning for your films."

"We're not sure yet; I'm still working on the proposals," I muttered into my glass.

"I'm sorry, darling, but with this towel around my hair I can barely hear

MY FARE LADY

you."

I resisted the urge to let my knowing smile escape to my lips. "I said we're working on our proposals; I'll get you copies when they're ready."

"I think I have an investor lined up but only if you are *sure* we can do them in Panama. Tell me a little about the first one, please?"

"I'd open up with Frank winging an old WW-II twin-engine bomber just yards above the waves to slip under Cuba's radar . . .," I started. I regurgitated my ideas about the retelling of Frank's adventurous life in enough detail to satisfy her.

"Holy Mother of God! Is this shit for real?" she stammered.

"Most of it, but remember we're not making a documentary here. I want to present Frank's character as an American James Bond."

"What sort of budget do you need to get started?"

I sighed and thought the question over for a moment. "I'd have to sign a director and our lead actor from the "A" list, you know, to get top-notch distribution. The good thing is that shooting off-shore should keep the overhead costs way low."

"Then Panama would be perfect; it even looks just like Cuba!" She cooed.

"Panama? Do they even have a studio big enough?"

"If not, we'll build one. But Bobby, here's the key question: if I get you the financing there, wouldn't our films be considered foreign products?"

"Only if we did everything through a Panamanian corporation," I answered honestly.

"That's what I wanted to hear. Listen, darling Bobby," she cooed again, "this must be our secret for now, right? Don't even tell Frank until I get things set. OK?"

"Er, sure, but what if . . .," I stammered.

"Leave it there, Bobby-boy," she winked, draining *both* of our glasses.

"But why would your people want to *build* a studio there?" I asked, legitimately curious.

"Oh, darling, my friend and his family are very, very close to El Presidente Omar Torrijos of Panama. El Presidente's brother controls the banks, and those banks hold a *ton* of money for my friend's extended family. So, the issue has been that they have to get that money back some way and keep the benefit for the family," she said, getting to her feet and wobbling toward the bedroom door.

"Now excuse me," she purred, "but I must check my service one last time before I get zonked. Just wait, please. I don't want you to cut out without giving me a goodnight kiss!"

I did something that rarely happens; I blushed.

I had no doubts remaining. I was included in every bit of this potential plot because of my relationship with Frank. My mind shifted into 100 percent business mode. The facts that I had were that Piazza and his crew could use all the money they could get offshore to create a foreign film, import it, and then *legitimately* declare its profits here in the United States. They could launder dirty money milked from drugs, gambling, and prostitution as squeaky-clean as new blown snow. My mind roared at me to hold up and come about. The biggest mystery is how they got their money *out* in the first place. If I could uncover *that* link . . .

My mind drifted down that train of though for a mere moment before my greedy side started hissing, "*Hush up, you idiot!* Forget that quixotic horseshit; this could be the answer to all your aspirations. Yessir," that voice cooed, "if you play your cards right, you would be on the ground floor. So what would it hurt to play along a bit longer, say a year or two?" The greedy yet somehow soothing voice in my head had a good point. I could pull the plug at any time I chose.

My thoughts froze as I heard Olga's muffled scream. Before I could move, she rushed in and started pulling me to the door.

"Get out, Bobby! *Hurry, hurry, hurry*! Take the stairs; go out through the garage! Stay off the street and use the bushes! Run! *Run!*" she gasped.

"What's happening–," I tried to question.

"Get out!" she shrieked.

It was enough motivation, regardless of the confusion and motive. I took the stairs two at a time and made it to my car. Had Butch and his crew realized my plans? How could they know? Or was Olga putting on an act to get me out where they could . . . do *what* exactly?

Maggie Mae rode shotgun with me while we circled through the darkest

MY FARE LADY

side streets Coral Gables offered. Once certain I was alone and hadn't been tailed, I returned, cruising past the David William. I looked toward her living quarters. Every light in her apartment was ablaze, so I slipped back into the parking garage. I climbed the stairs, Maggie Mae in hand, two at a time and ghosted to her door. She was jabbering so hysterically I could not distinguish a single word. I strained to make out some details of what transpired but couldn't. Afraid of blowing my cover, I conceded defeat. Maggie and I went home to spend a restless night.

Crap!

The morning headlines on April 7, 1977, announced that the U.S. District Court in Atlanta, Georgia, had indicted Miami's newly appointed "Most Eligible Bachelor," none other than John Charles Piazza III, and his mother, Cora "Coco" Piazza, on racketeering and interstate drug-trafficking charges. DEA warrants also were issued for several members of their crew, including one Michael Centoducati, my recently found suspect endearingly referred to as Mikey Ducks. One glance at his photo confirmed Frank's suspicion: Mikey Ducks *was* my Porsche-boy from the Monkey Jungle parking lot.

It appeared that my ambition to become the scourge of the Florida Mafia (or its movie mogul?) was over. I didn't allow myself time to pout, so I shifted my attention back to my *Taxi* proposal and started planning for a quick visit to Los Angeles to see what I could set up. Later that evening I was surprised by a call from Olga, whom I had already started writing off as recent history.

Over what sounded like mall noises, I gathered that if I was *really* her friend and if I *really* wanted to get my films financed, she needed a *big* favor. Her directions were explicit.

CITIZEN SPY

At precisely ten o'clock that evening, I must park on any side street near the David William. I must enter through the lobby and take the elevator to the fourth floor. Instead of getting off, I then must punch the button to the floor below. If no one was in the hallway, I was to get off and take the stairs back down to the parking garage. However, if I encounter so much as a blind woman in a wheelchair I must repeat everything until I make it into that garage unseen. Once there, I should hurry to the last row on the south side of that garage and look for a powder-blue Ford sedan bearing an Avis rental sticker.

Everything went according to plan, yet the sedan appeared as empty as last Sunday's collection plate. The sound of running feet made me whip my head around. It was nearly impossible to recognize the usually meticulously neat, clean, and chic Olga. She wore no makeup, no lipstick, her hair hung in tangled strands, and her jogging suit was a rumpled mess.

"Please, *please*, Morgan! You have to help me," she gasped. "I promised Butch we could trust you for sure. Oh, God, I've never been so scared! Where did you park?"

"Next street over. I saw the newspapers, I'm sorry . . . " I trailed off, not exactly sure what I was sorry for.

Hands trembling, she dropped her keys twice before she managed to open the car's trunk. Inside were a battered old suitcase secured by a tangled web of knotted clothesline, a five-foot-long metal-and-wood apparatus secured by twin straps, and a twelve-inch by fourteen-inch packet tightly bound by layers of duct tape. It tipped over and fell with a metallic clunk.

"What's this rig?" I asked as we extracted the long apparatus and the suitcase.

"That's Butch's old printing thing-a-ma-jig. Can you take it and that suitcase, too?" she asked, snatching up the packet and stuffing it under her jacket. I didn't move, unsure if I wanted to jump back into her game after spending my day thinking I had jumped out.

MY FARE LADY

Who was I kidding? I was there with her and that was answer enough.

"Please, Bobby, take those two out to the Everglades, I know you know the best spots. Bury them where they'll *never* be found. I'll call you, I promise."

Without another word, she turned, jogging out of sight as I just stood, watching.

I drove home, unable to resist a quick peek at what in the hell was in that suitcase. I sawed into its bindings and snapped the lock open with a screwdriver. The damned thing was stuffed with boxes of ammunition, a flashy chrome-plated Arminius .38 revolver, and a pearl-handled Llama .45 ACP pistol.

She wanted me to ditch two fine weapons like that? Not likely!

Instead, I stashed everything behind my water tank, plunked a half-dozen bricks inside the suitcase, tossed it in atop the "printing thing-a-ma-jig" and took off across the Everglades.

It was close to 3 a.m. before my cargo and I reached the fishing village of Chokoloskee, some eighty miles west of Miami. Switching off my headlights, I puttered slowly down Mamie Street, past clusters of darkened cottages. When I reached the last dock, I padded out to its end and pitched that suitcase one way and the printer the other. Even if some angler should snag them, who would make a big deal about dredging up a suitcase of bricks and a piece of unwieldy junk?

Thankfully, I had Wolfman Jack's radio show "spinning the platters" keeping me company on the long ride home.

Over the ensuing weeks, I focused my attention on the test-market release of my upcoming film. When the reviews came in, they were encouraging. Having the security of good reviews in hand, I made reservations to leave for Los Angeles to begin courting major distributors. I was feeling on top of the world. My elation, however, was short lived. An oddly chirpy and cheerful Olga called, announcing that she had wonderful, just *wonderful* news, so would I *please* take her to see my film at the Coral Way Drive-in Theater?

I asked her when and she said she wanted to go that very evening, of course. Moreover, she had a "special friend" who wanted to meet me as per our–*insert polite "ahem" here*–future plans. She asked me to pick her up at her new suite at the David William an hour before sundown.

This was Olga. How could I possibly refuse?

A single tap at her door brought Olga. She slipped out, perhaps more akin to *slithered* out, slamming the door immediately behind her. As guarded and hasty as she had been, I still managed to catch a scant glimpse through the door. That glance into her new suite made a profound impression. Unlike her previous suite, this was a morass of wadded clothing, overflowing ashtrays, empty beer cans, and scattered fast-food sacks. I was mystified. The entire scene was completely out of character for her; most particularly a rumpled Miami Dolphin's sweatsuit and crushed ball cap that centered that mess.

She gave me no time to ask or think, hustling me down to the garage to yet another rented sedan. Olga made it a point to coo that our special guest must have the entire backseat to himself and asked, in that molten chocolate voice of hers, if I minded driving. My imagination flashed to the recent *Godfather* film where the walking dead sat in the front seat while their assassin crouched behind them. I casually shifted Maggie May to the left side of my jacket, hopefully out of Olga's reach, and swore to myself that should anyone so much as wriggle . . .

The safety-conscious voice in my head had had enough. What was I doing here? I should be taking my Emily out for Chinese food instead of hanging out with criminals! In fact, I should be *anywhere* but here.

I pushed the voice out of earshot.

Olga and I cruised west along Coral Way until she ordered a sudden left turn onto De Soto. At the Venetian Pool we veered south on Toledo to Anastasia and made two more lefts and a quick right, bringing us right back in the David William garage.

"Slow down, slow down!" she rasped, gesturing for me to back off with her hands.

"OK, real slow," she whispered as a thick figure, clad in that Miami Dolphins sweatsuit I had spied in her suite, rose from the shadows, jerked open the door, dived into the backseat, somehow managing to shut the door on the fly, and flattened out of sight. Once again, Olga directed me to play ring-around-the-backstreets of Coral Gables until she said, "OK, you can sit up now, Mikey."

MY FARE LADY

The face that appeared in my rearview mirror was none other than Michael Centoducati, known on the streets and in certain circles as "Pie," or "Mikey Ducks." Indeed, it became apparent that Miami's "Most Wanted" fugitive was now my "special guest" for a night at the movies. Somehow, worse, he was the Porsche-driving son of a bitch I had seen getting his take from the drug supplier to my Emily's schoolyard.

Wise words spoken to me long ago by my adoptive father, Nino Cochise, echoed in my mind: "Always be the hunter, my son; never the prey."

I refused all offers to pay our way into the drive-in theater and I supplied all the double-cheeseburgers, fries, colas, and milkshakes they could stuff down their gullets. Why? I was sure that Olga would be paying with money from Mikey . . . money I knew might have been be some kid's lunch money. The thought made my stomach roil.

Watching my own film, *Bloodstalkers*, felt somehow ironic. For various reasons, I ended up acting in the movie as well. My role was that of a cold-blooded and sadistic killer. I felt the sheer irony as I watched my portrayal of a criminal while a real one, breathing down my neck and rooting for my villainous character, was sitting in my backseat.

Outing ended, we returned to Olga's messy apartment for more of her special vodka martinis. After three or four rounds, Olga asked if I had taken care of Butch's suitcase and printing press. I assured her everything was swimming with sharks in salty waters.

"Oh, Morgan! I can't believe you fell for that!" she jested. "We were only *testing* you. Mikey had put a bunch of rocks in that old suitcase. Isn't he just too funny?"

"Yeah, and you did good, man. Real good," Mikey grunted and grinned.

"Say, *what*? You had me drive all that way, in the middle of the night, to pitch a bunch of rocks and that freaking printing press just to *test* me? What the . . . up yours, man!" I glared, playing my role flawlessly.

"Aw, it was one of Butch's toys; he won't need it for a while," Mikey laughed.

"Screw both of you," I yelled, feigning a perfect tantrum, "and lose my number!" I launched myself toward the door but, mid-stride, Olga grabbed one arm and Mikey pinned the other.

"Whoa, hey, lighten up, man," he chuckled, guiding me back to the couch. "We had to check, you know, OK? And thanks for gettin' me out of here tonight. I was goin' nuts."

I allowed Olga to refresh my drink.

"Yeah, sure, OK," I sighed, "I'll give you that one shot, but any more crap like that and I'm gone for good."

"You have our word, right, Mikey?" Olga purred.

"Yeah, yeah, right. So let's talk about this movie shit. Tell him, Olga."

Olga virtually glowed; she was so excited to share her news. "Listen, we know who to talk to for the studio, the money, everything!" she said, too evenly for it to be a lie.

"Trust me, man," Mikey added, "you play us straight and I'll always watch your back all the way, understand?"

They spent the next hour outlining how I needed to meet someone named Mark who owned resort hotels in Aspen, a tennis village near Orlando, and was making a fortune renting his fleet of yachts for private parties. They were sure he was the perfect front for us. Besides, he had connections in a new distribution company.

"Mark's over in Tampa now picking up another yacht," Olga said. "We'd go over but he's having all sorts of toys built into it. He's like a little kid when it comes to details. We'll get with him when you're back from LA so we can partner up, OK, Bobby?"

My inner ambitious voice screamed at me over and over again to lose my morals as they went on describing this Mark character. He was an early investor in New Line Cinema, a fresh independent film distribution company out of New York that imported foreign films from innovative directors such as that new German genius Werner Herzog. That little voice in my head was yelling–no, *wailing*–that such an introduction might prove to be my breakthrough. I had to get that side of me under control. This was how people lost it, lost *themselves* in a world of corruption. No matter that how much I sprinkled on the sugar, the facts remained that this, or any other favor Mikey spoke of, must be counted as coming from the Mafia.

Olga's whisper in my ear tugged me back to the table.

". . . and Bobby, be sure to call when you leave Los Angeles so I can arrange a meeting with Mark. Then, if it all goes right, we'll probably have to jet down to Panama to get the ball rolling for your studio."

"Panama? Why Panama?"

"You said you had films you could do there."

"Well, sure, but why not shoot the first one here? The Everglades are perfect for..."

"It's there or no deal, Morgan. Trust me; we have our reasons. Yes or no? We can make a lot of money together. A *lot*," she said, putting a distinct emphasis that made dollar signs roll through my mind's eye, "but we have to go where it is."

I drained my drink and headed for the door. "I'll call you when I get back," I promised, but I secretly hoped I would never see either of them again. I was terrified that I was losing myself. I didn't know if I could keep up the charade or if I was going to give in to the lure of easy money and realized dreams. For the first time, I really questioned whether I had the character, the moral fortitude I knew I needed for this potentially deadly game of cat and mouse.

5 THE RAT'S NEST

Hollywood fell short of my expectations and my *Taxi* proposal was still on hold. Disgusted and dejected, I returned to Miami on a late flight. I was unlocking my door when I heard Olga's panicked voice on my answering machine, pleading that I rush straightaway to her apartment the moment I arrived, no matter what the time.

Here we go again, I thought. I asked myself if I should ignore her or call back to tell her to lose my number? But what if her deal worked out; why shoot myself in the foot if I didn't know why she was calling?

I arrived at her door just shy of midnight and barely tapped it before she squirted out, shoving me down the hall to a corner niche. Her report was grim; the courts had allowed Butch's mother, Coco, to make bail but had denied his. Tonight "they" needed my help because most of the members of their usual crews were behind bars, had left the state, or were in hiding.

"It's so bad that even Morris is here," she whispered.

"Who?" I asked, racking my mental repositories for the name.

"Morris Kerr! He's with *Lansky*," she hissed, turning to give the door a quick glance.

"As in Meyer–"

"Shhhh!" she spat, turning back to face me. "He's one of his top attorneys. And don't say anything about Freddy, OK? Morris is his father . . ."

"Freddy?"

". . . and let *me* do the talking," she said, shoving me inside her suite and

THE RAT'S NEST

double locking the door behind us, click-click.

The first person I spied was a woman I guessed to be in her sixties, made top-heavy with layers of garish necklaces, pendants, bracelets, and studded rings. She was busy emptying filing cabinets of folders and stacking them onto Olga's long dining room table. At the head of the table, a grim-faced man was hunched over, thumbing through each folder to sort its content into twin stacks. The papers to his left were waiting to be stashed into cardboard filing boxes; the stack to his right was being shoved into huge plastic lawn bags. The only sounds beyond shuffling papers and sliding drawers came from a back bedroom where a paper cutter was methodically chop-chop-chopping.

I noted, too, that every window was draped shut with thick blankets, concealing even the dimmest light.

Morris Kerr's London-cut silk suit with an Allen Solly shirt and tie, diamond-ringed Rolex Oyster Perpetual wristwatch and matching cuff links advertised him as an expensive legal-beagle, but his constant scowl warned that he would consider it an insult if a stranger thought him friendly. What made the picture ludicrous was the white cotton gloves he wore to hide his fingerprints.

"This is our friend, Morgan," Olga said as she ushered me into the room. "He's the one that I told you about. He was in LA on movie business and just got back. He came right over to help."

The older woman waggled one bejeweled hand my way. "Heard some good shit about you, kid," she said in a husky, long-time smoker's voice. "I'm Butch's mother; you can call me Coco. The sourpuss over there is—"

"He doesn't need to know," Morris snapped.

Clearly embarrassed, Coco sniffed, "He's always crabby, Morgan. I'll bet he hasn't smiled since his mother stopped changing his diapers."

"Shut your trap, Coco! Your idiot son got too damned greedy and made side deals for what?! Pennies? Now look at the mess you're in. If it was my call, I'd let you both fry!"

"Morris, please! I'm sure this will all fade away," Coco pleaded.

"Stop with the names already," he snapped back. "I know you're dumb, but are you deaf, too?"

CITIZEN SPY

For a brief moment, I felt sorry for her. The empathy was short lived; I remembered that addicts young and old had paid for every piece of her gewgaw.

I took a harder look at Morris Kerr, inspecting him while trying to look nonchalantly at the operation of which I was now involved. I noticed then what he kept near his elbow. *Damn!* It told me all I needed know about this hired legal beagle. There were four open squirt cans of lighter fluid poised beside a silver-and-gold cigarette lighter, yet there were neither cigarettes nor ashtrays in sight. My imagination flashed a grisly scenario: at the first sound of a fist or a crowbar at the door, Morris could do some fast squirt-squirts from the cans, a snap-snap of a lighter, and whoosh—an instant inferno would devour their secrets.

This creature, masquerading as a human being, was willing to set fire to an entire hotel filled with sleeping innocents to protect his—or *their*—rotten asses.

Tasked to help cram all the "to save" files into the filing boxes, I worked without speaking for a full hour before making a trip to the bathroom. As I passed through the master bedroom, I discovered it was Mikey Ducks operating the paper guillotine. While he gave me a quick embrace, which was either sincerely friendly or to check for a wire, I noted his victims were crisp new treasury notes. My memory of Butch's newly water-bound portable printing press provided the answer—they were phony.

It was nearing dawn before Morris completed his inspection of every cabinet, file, drawer, crack, and crevice in the apartment before making a whispered telephone call.

"Is it safe? OK, give us another fifteen minutes and then shut down," he said, hanging up the phone. "Mike!" he barked, "You know what to do so make sure you get it done." Still wearing gloves, Morris Kerr, Esq., stalked out without a grunt, a thank you, or even a paltry kiss-my-ass.

A sobering thought flashed through my mind: did he have someone watching the David William? Worse, did he have a snitch inside the Dade County Task Force? If so, that would explain why the fuzz so easily lost Olga's taxi rides. It was at that moment that I decided when the time came to shut this game down, I would not chance talking with the local law enforcement but would deal only with the DEA. These people started this game of cat and mouse for me by bringing drugs to Emily's school . . . so the DEA would be my choice to close their shop.

We all scrambled to ferry the filing boxes and trash bags to the underground parking garage where twin U-Haul vans were parked. We stashed the "to-save" boxes in one, and Olga and Coco climbed aboard and disappeared into the night. Mikey and I jammed all the bags of chaff and castoff files into the remaining van.

"If bright-boy Morris Kerr was so damned careful," I wondered aloud, "maybe we should've worn gloves, too?"

Mikey answered in the cliché fashion that has become Hollywood mafia. "Fuhgeddaboudit," he smiled, "this crap'll be smoke before the sun shines."

I tossed in the last two bags and said, "It's all yours, Mikey. See you later."

"Whoa, man; you're drivin'! There ain't no traffic and the cops are lookin' for me everywhere," he said, burrowing in among the bags.

He was correct. Civilian traffic was nonexistent, but I did pass two cruisers.

When we pulled into the deserted Dinner Key Marina, it was not hard to spot the two burly men lounging at the end of one dock. Within minutes, we four had hustled our cargo onto the deck of a sleek Bertram cabin cruiser. My gut went taut when I spied a lidless fifty-five-gallon drum lashed to its afterdeck in between a case of beer, an ice chest, and a huge bucket of Kentucky Fried Chicken. That drum bothered me; at five-foot-eight and 165 pounds, I could fit inside easily.

My fears proved groundless. Once loaded, the thugs clambered aboard, started the engines, and flipped twin birds at Mikey and me as they rumbled away.

En route back to the David William, I violated one of Frank's rules by asking Mikey about that empty drum. I admitted that I thought it might have been for me.

"Maybe next time," he laughed. "Nah, they're heading out to one of those sand spits to make it look like they've had an all-night beer-bust. They'll use that drum to burn up all that crap and the fuzz'll think they're roasting weenies."

"Do you mind if I ask another question?"

"Too many ain't smart, Bobby-boy," Mikey responded.

"It's about Olga."

"Well, she ain't no friggin' virgin if that's what you're asking," he offered, laughing.

"With all the heat from the cop shop, how come her apartment hasn't been searched before now?"

"You mean where we were tonight? Who said it was hers?"

"Er," I stammered, "it's the only place I've been . . ."

"Oh, come on, wise up, man," he replied, obviously stunned at my naivete. "We've got lots of 'em leased under all kinds of names. Listen, listen; if that broad ever takes you to her personal pad, you'd better wear a seat belt or she'll buck your skinny ass clean through the ceiling."

I took his warning to heart. Looking back, I thank God I never had to follow it. Ironically, from that night forward, I never heard another word about Mikey Ducks. It was as if he had simply vanished.

After the night of "cleaning house," I became Olga's designated chauffeur to and from the airport while she made a flurry of damage-control missions in the wake of Piazza's arrest. Her destinations: New York, Chicago, Cincinnati, New Orleans, Atlanta, Los Angeles, Las Vegas, Aspen, San Francisco, Houston, Tucson, Curacao, Caracas, Nassau, Mexico City, Hermosillo, Guayamas, and Panama City. If nothing else, she was a well-traveled woman.

I also kept badgering her about our venture to create the film studio in Panama. I was curious whether her friends' risk capital dried up because the DEA was roasting Piazza's goose. Quite the opposite was true, she assured me. She had been reassigned and was leaving soon to work directly with Morris's son, Fred. Better yet, Morris had resolved his former reservations about me and had turned our studio idea over to Olga and Fred with his blessing.

In fact, Fred had already obtained copies of the documentary Bostonia Film Productions had made about my 1971 American Yeti Expedition and he knew, too, that my most recent film was doing well at that year's Cannes Film Festival.

THE RAT'S NEST

Then, when Olga told Morris that I had a contract with Sturgis and Oscar Fraley to makes films about Frank's adventures in Cuba, he had all the endorsements he needed. He decided he would arrange the financing to create a *true* film studio for the new venture in Panama, but it would be my responsibility to select our film projects and to oversee the studio's day-to-day functions.

After another evening of endless rounds of vodka martinis, Olga began babbling that she was sure that millions of dollars of Mafia money was being smuggled out of the States to Italy. From Italy, the money somehow traveled to South America and then returned to the States, fully laundered, ready for investing in all sorts of legitimate businesses. When I raised a curious eyebrow, she expounded that the general businesses were malls and housing projects all over Southern California and Arizona.

She bragged that this was the "exactly-for-sure-honest-to-God" method preferred by the Mafia to launder money. "See, see, see," she giggled, "that's why our Panama thingy would fit in perfectly!"

She swore giddily that we were "in" and added, "oh, by the way, my new boss Freddy-baby asked that you help me perform a personal favor for him."

Again, I raised a questioning eyebrow. She told me that my favor was to accompany her on a mission wherein I would use my "Jarvis glare," a reference to my character in *Bloodstalkers*, to intimidate someone to whom Freddy bore a huge grudge. I asked when and she merely stated that the sooner the better. Curious about the mission and whom I would be staring down on behalf of the Mafia, I asked if the next day was too soon.

Olga beamed.

Naturally, I assumed our target would be male. All the movies, media, and books I knew regarding the Mafia made it clear that *men* got in trouble and needed outside staredowns.

I was wrong.

Our quarry was a petite, blonde woman whose initial sin, it seemed, was becoming Fred Kerr's wife. Her second sin was being mother to his only son. Her third, objecting to how he made his living as a gangster. And her final one was divorcing him and refusing his visitation rights.

CITIZEN SPY

The next afternoon I donned my actual "Jarvis wardrobe" to escort Olga to an exclusive *haute couture* dress shop in the heart of Coconut Grove. My assignment was to block the door while she delivered Freddy's message by dropping, dragging, and trampling thousand-dollar designer dresses, being sure to ruin them.

When the former Mrs. Kerr finally dialed the cop shop, we leered and sneered and slithered away.

Safe again, Olga asked, "Know what we have to do tomorrow? Fred wants us to meet his friend Mark for lunch in Key West. Pick me up before nine o'clock and dress nice. He's a New Yorker and big on first impressions." She started to turn away and stopped. "Oh, I almost forgot. We need to pick up a pizza for Mikey. Want to come up for dinner?"

"I have a date."

Her eyebrows lifted nearly to her hairline.

"Anybody I know?"

"It's my night with my daughter and it's always a twosome.

It was unfathomable. In a single afternoon, I had gone from acting the ugly jerk, menacing a frightened owner of a dress shop, to just another proud papa escorting his daughter to her ethnic dancing class in Coconut Grove. My bipolar transition was too damned smooth and too damned easy. Moreover, my gentle child who loved bugs, fish, animals, snakes, birds, bats, and all things great and small seemed not to notice a single difference in her doting papa.

What strange creatures we humans are. Is this how those "made members" of the Mafia act after committing murders on command? Do they consider themselves cold-blooded killers or normal parents? On the other hand, it could be that the duplicity, the dual-personality trait that seems special to them . . . was now me?

My guts twisted at that thought until the music started and I watched Emily take her place on the floor. I always felt content watching her dance. I was no longer the guy trying to get an "in" with the Mafia simply to destroy what I could

THE RAT'S NEST

from the inside, yet the reason for my contentedness was the reason behind my ploy.

I watched her, lost in what I was willing to do to keep her safe. She was as graceful as a fresh breeze and had this way of flipping her silky hair in perfect cadence to the traditional Middle Eastern music. I stood in wonder when she responded to each drumbeat or woodwind wail as if slumbering genes were stirring within her most secret being. I, on the other hand, shuffled around a dance floor like a three-legged and all-left-footed *klutz* as she captivated everyone with her huge and happy smile.

As was our wont, we followed her lessons with munchies at Lum's Restaurant and then, hand-in-hand, we strolled through the myriad of tourist shops. How nice it was; how carefree to have no worries of being discovered, no questioning the point behind large barrels, no fear of sleeping residents burning in the night. We seldom bought anything as we strolled; we just looked while she chattered on about her friends, her school, her classes, boys, and all the other stuff about which dads and daughters gab.

However, as we passed the park that night, we caught a whiff of sweet smoke. Emily whispered, too knowingly, "That's *pot*, Dad," and went on to ask if I had tried it.

I replied that I had not and would not because I wanted nothing that would alter my natural moods or my thought processes, nor did I want anything in my lungs except air. I then bridged into the wisdom of healthy eating and balancing "good" carbohydrates with "good" oils and "good" proteins.

"But you drink alcohol sometimes," she said solemnly.

"True, but I usually limit myself to red wines, which have some health benefits. When you are older, I will introduce you to the better ones, OK?"

"Did you ever get drunk," she giggled.

"Once," I smiled back.

"Tell me about it. Please, please?"

"Well, Nosy-Rosy, I was in the Navy and my ship was docked at Subic Bay in the Philippines. It was super hot and muggy, we had just cruised up from Bangkok through the South China Sea, and one of our water evaporators had shut down. Think about it; two thousand sailors had no showers for more than a week. Boy, oh, boy, when we hit the beach we guzzled all the San Miguel beers we could find. No one told us that domestic Filipino beer was treated with formaldehyde. Know what that is?"

"Nope," Emily said with owlishly curious eyes.

"It's that embalming fluid undertakers put into dead bodies to preserve them."

"Yuk. Why did they do that to beer?"

"Something about the temperature in the tropics, I guess. Anyway, my head hurt for a week. I've never let that happen again, no matter what."

"Did you have a good time, though?"

"Not really. Being drunk is . . . well, I guess you could say its second- or third-class happiness. What you and I are doing now are the best times I'll ever have for all my life," I said, prancing around her to make her laugh. "See how pretty I am even at my advanced age. Maybe I should get some more San Miguel's so I can stay this way."

Emily laughed, hugging me and saying she loved it best when I clowned for her, but then my child unwittingly opened a Pandora's Box that would never completely close for either of us.

"But Dad, the kids at school are saying that marijuana is a natural plant and it's been around for thousands of years and it really makes you learn better because it keeps you from getting all stressed out over grades and stuff . . ."

God help me, and perhaps one day Emily may understand and forgive me, but I felt something explode inside my skull. The thought of some slime-ball street-dealing son of a bitch filling her head with that crap flooded me with more hatred than I thought could exist within the bounds of a single human body. One moment I was a five-foot-eight, 165-pound average guy; my next breath swelled me into a six-foot-nine, 320-pound Mongol that nothing short of a tank-killer round could have stopped from ripping out their corrupt hearts and eating them raw.

Looking back, I'm willing to admit that perhaps marijuana, in and of itself, might provide positive benefits to specific medical, physical, and psychological needs. Perhaps one day it might be fully legal. In truth, I had never heard of any violent crime committed under its influence. Nevertheless, I knew that cheap weed was the lost-leader used by dealers to hook kids on to the hard stuff and that would put nails in their coffins for life.

"Listen to me, goddamn it," I heard myself roaring at my child. "If you need to get rid of stress, take up tap-dancing, yodeling, or running track for crying out loud! Don't you ever put anything into your body except the most healthful foods you can find! Not pot, not pills, not drugs, and don't you *ever* use needles. Do you hear me?"

"Y-yes, Dad. I-I didn't mean . . ., " she started crying.

"Doesn't your school teach you how your lungs are supposed to work? To stay alive and healthy you have to breathe in the cleanest air you can find so your body can extract the good oxygen and exchange it for stuff you need to get rid of, right? Every time you let smoke or fumes of any kind get in your lungs, you are coating them with *crap*. On top of that, pot is a *drug*! Do you understand me? *Do you?*"

"Yessss, Dad, *b-but* . . . " she tried to continue.

"Why do you think it's against the law? Drugs are supposed to be used to fight diseases and not for stupid-ass recreation!"

"I-I didn't say that, Dad. I-I just asked. I'm sorry, I'm sorry," she said, whimpering.

Oh, God! Was that *fear* I saw creeping into her eyes? Fear . . . of *me*? I would walk forever over broken glass in bare feet before knowingly causing pain to my daughter, and here she was, looking at me like I was scaring her to death. How was she ever going to want to talk to me, to be open with me, if even the *subject* of drugs was insidious and poisonous?

We did not say much as we made walked back to my car and drove to her mother's apartment. Later that night, our happy mood ripped to shreds, I masked my pain by singing her favorite song until she soothed away to slumber land.

I waited until her hand curled into its favorite snuggle-spot beneath her chin before slipping away. It was hard to accept that when the upcoming school year began, she would be a freshman in high school. Where, oh where does time go?

CITIZEN SPY

While returning to my hovel, my mind was made up. No more internally questioning my own motives; no more letting the greedy, ambitious business side of me take the floor. A phrase I read somewhere set my course: "Keep your friends close, but your enemies closer."

Frank and Eddie's lectures rang true and finally hit home. They were right; taking down corner dealers was useless. The true demons were the brains behind the entire operation. My war, if there was to be one, must be up close and personal and my attack must come when least expected.

I wasn't exactly sure how I would get close enough. I knew step one was already done. Step two would mean I accepted Olga's overtures on the morrow to join the soulless bastards and ingratiate myself into their league.

6 FREDDY-BABY

It was another hot and muggy drive from Miami to the southernmost terminus of U.S. Highway 1 in Key West. It did not take long to discover that our trip was *not* about meeting this Mark character but more because Olga wanted time alone to define our mutual interests in the Panama film studio venture.

She opened the topic by promising that if I handled the day-to-day business, she would act as my listening post with the bosses. She advised that I should not get nosy about who the investors were, where the money was coming from, or who was handling the sales or distribution. I was a *contractor*, not a partner, and I was to negotiate the amount I would be paid.

She further told me that I must not ask for anything on the backend or expect to participate in the film's profits. She would serve as my eyes and ears among her associates and, in return, I must cut her in on my end.

"That sounds like about 5 percent of what I net," I said. "No, let's make it an even 10 percent," sounding generous.

"Dream on," she laughed. "Without me you don't have a deal."

"Make it fifteen," I smiled.

"Twenty-five," she countered.

"Twenty or no deal," I offered.

"Next time over I'll set up accounts for us in Switzerland," she said.

"Why?" I asked.

"Oh, darling," she purred, "why pay income taxes if you don't *have* to? Just jet over like everyone else any time you need cash."

"So tell me about this what's-his-name we're supposed to meet?"

Throughout the duration of the remaining trip, I learned that "Mark F." was a popular New York playboy but had become the mob's pawn because he ran up gambling debts he could not pay. Instead of dropping him into the East River, they were kind enough to give him an offer he could not refuse. He was investing their money in the trendiest New York nightclubs, but always in his own name. He also had arranged to skim the till of said clubs. Moreover, he was responsible for luring the most politically powerful men among his free-spending "beautiful people" to the trendiest places that were, of course, owned or controlled by the Mafia.

The new yacht that Mark was sailing north also had a special purpose. It was to be made freely available to certain high-profile targets the Mafia would select because every inch of living space had been custom wired to record private and intimate conversations. Better yet, the yacht's skipper could operate spy cameras concealed in the main stateroom and every sleeping quarter to film the hanky-panky between Mark's guests and his paid party girls. Nothing like a little blackmail material sitting in the wings for a rainy day.

Another interesting gadget on the captain's control panel would alert him if some smart guest used a detection device.

Olga also shared that every dime fed through the Mafia's pipeline appeared to pass through someone she only knew as "the General," but its final destination was controlled by a phantom they referred to as "the Judge."

Olga's guess was that the General was either Meyer Lansky, Butch's father in Atlanta, or *his* boss, Carlos Marcello in New Orleans. She admitted that the one termed the Judge remained a mystery even to her, but her bet was on Joseph Bonanno.

"If this Mark character is a nobody, why the hell are we going all the way to Key West in this heat?" I asked.

FREDDY-BABY

"Because we're alone and we can talk without someone taping us," she answered bluntly. "But I also heard he has some personal connections that could help get your films distributed worldwide."

"So let's make our drive a two-way street," I said. "Tell me who the good sharks are versus the bad ones who love nothing more than the smell of fresh blood in the water."

By the time we reached Tavernier, I found out that Butch Piazza's father was a true capo and had major social status and influence in Atlanta, and he was *super* pissed at the way John was acting. However, the real "juice" came directly from Carlos Marcello, the top dog in New Orleans. When I heard that bit of news, I had New York's top-cop Eddie Egan's words ringing in my ears: "*Marcello is a powerful man and a killer from the get-go. And remember that he and Butch Piazza's old man are in tight with Joe Bonanno.*"

Olga snapped me back to the present when she added that because she was now Fred Kerr's number one assistant, she was in a position to help our side action at every turn.

We had barely made Key West when Olga spotted our target fussing about his flashy new yacht. I could tell Mark wasn't my type of guy from first glance. He was a mushy, soft sort and reeked of scents too sweet to be considered manly. Worse, he opened our conversation by bragging about owning a tennis village near Orlando, a ski resort in Aspen, and insinuating that I *must* know that his Big Apple nightspots were always crammed with jet-set swingers.

When he finally paused to take a breath, Olga asked if it was true that he knew some of the folks at New Line Cinema. At the time, New Line Cinema was a fresh and quite legitimate film distribution company. He told her that yes, he did and then expounded by again bragging that they often came to one of his nightclubs.

Olga smiled a conspiratorial smile and asked Mark if he could keep a huge secret. Certain people they both knew—as in Freddy You-Know-Who—intended to make several of my feature films offshore. Naturally, we would be looking for distribution but preferred to deal outside Hollywood. Therefore, since Mark had admitted he was pals with certain unnamed people at New Line, couldn't we expect an honest payback? Especially if he gave us his personal guarantee.

Mark's shoulders hunched forward and his hands began massaging one another as if they were lovers. She had played him perfectly and we all knew it. He agreed that our idea about producing a sequence of films offshore was "fabulous," and yes, he promised that the moment he reached New York he would ask one of New Line's executives to contact us.

Olga and I left Mark pacing about his yacht with the shared opinion that he was otherwise useless and she needed to get me in direct contact with Fred in Los Angeles as soon as possible. Curious, I asked when that was going to be and she stunned me by asking me if I would *please* take her to the airport the following morning.

A full month passed during which I learned the definition to the term "limbo." I can deal with discussions and an occasional argument, but I bloody-well hate silence. Thankfully, my time in limbo ended when Sturgis telephoned, asking me to pick him up at the Miami International Airport that evening. He said that, by chance, he had encountered Olga at some Holiday Inn in New York while she was en route to perform yet another courier mission to South America. Apparently, he had message for me.

Frank bolted out of the terminal, tossed his suitcase my way, and announced that he wanted supper at one of his back-alley haunts in Little Havana. En route, he informed me that Olga permanently vacated her apartment at the David William. I turned, shocked at the news. He continued, saying I could rest assured that everything was happening exactly as she and I had planned. He then presented me with the business card of one Frederick Kerr, Esq., of Newport Beach, California. Scrawled on the back was a short note indicating he was expecting my call.

Frank spent an entire evening warning me that I was adrift in deep waters, waters he didn't know if I could successfully navigate, but then assuring me that I had his ear anytime, anywhere.

The following day, I learned that Quinn Martin Productions had passed on my *Taxi* proposal in lieu of something called *Miami Vice*. I placed a call to Frederick Kerr. At his invitation, I hopped in the car for the ultra-long drive West, ready for a nose-to-nose sit-down.

FREDDY-BABY

I arrived at Newport Beach's upscale Promontory Point Apartments to "do lunch" with Olga and Fred. I barely touched the buzzer before the door flew open and there stood Morris Kerr's favorite son. As this was California's prime yuppie land, I had assumed his attire would be the usual silk shirt, a few heavy gold necklaces, crisp linen slacks, and Gucci loafers sans socks.

Instead, he wore crisp, new safari clothing complete with an ascot scarf and fresh-off-the-shelf Eddie Bauer hiking boots. For all his macho attire, his handshake was less than firm.

He had barely closed the door behind me before insisting that I "must, must, must" take him to the mountains in the Pacific Northwest where I had filmed *The Search for Bigfoot*. Worse, he wanted to make a film about this newly decided adventure. Thankfully, before he could set a date and somehow fast-talk me into committing to the project, a half-naked Olga popped around the corner, reminding "Freddy-baby" to tell me that his curmudgeonly father had given his nod to our partnership in the Panamanian film studio. The Kerrs, it seemed, would both form it and manage it for us.

While Olga disappeared to finish dressing, "Freddy-Baby" poured two double scotches to toast our future adventures. "After all," he said, "if handled correctly we will become a literal money pipeline for our funding partners."

He assured me with a knowing wink that they would be *quite* generous. Before I could ask him to expand on that pipeline comment, he commenced bragging that his father was on very close terms with Omar Torrijos, "El Presidente" of Panama. He beamed while he told me that the Torrijos family controlled several national banks–wink, wink.

"That's wonderful," I said without winking back.

"So how much do we need for our kick-off venture? And do you prefer Robert or Bob?"

"I always thought that one 'bobbed' for apples," I replied. "As to funds, let's assume 1.5 million dollars for the first in the series to see how it goes." He didn't bat an eyelash, so I continued. "But the actual budget can only come after we agree on the script and negotiate with the lead talent. I'll do my best to massage the script to fit existing locations so we can come in as low as possible."

"Olga said you'd just shot an entire feature for sixty thousand dollars," he countered.

"That is true, but misleading," I replied. "Both our cast and crew donated much of their time and equipment for a piece of the profits. Every actor and crewmember received only two thousand in cash, and that included me as its writer, director, co-producer, *plus* I carried a strong role. My partners, Irv Rudley and Stan Webb, tossed in the use of their recording studio and all the cameras, lighting, and sound equipment and they did the editing and the music. Everyone received an equal share as a cooperative effort, but had we paid even union scale minimums that film would have cost at least seven hundred fifty thousand dollars or more."

"Why did you do it that way?" he asked.

"It's all the cash we could raise because we were unknowns," I said.

"But isn't Panamanian labor cheap?" he prodded. "Plus I heard they have a shit pot full of actors."

"I'll use every talent we can find, but only if they fit the roles. Nevertheless, we'll need at least one or two lead actors who have a draw at the box-office. That talent, though . . . their agents will never let them appear on screen with rank amateurs," I said.

"But will we *really* need one-point-five mil?" he whined.

"Mr. Kerr," I said formally, "we won't know anything until we run the numbers. Believe me, I'll keep the scripts as tight as possible, but it's imperative that our first venture makes a splash at the box office. The better the reviews, the more profits we can expect. Maybe your friend Mark could work something out with New Line?"

"Forget that clown," he sneered. "Ever hear of Josef Shaftel? He produced *The Naked Hills*, *Where Does It Hurt*, and *The Untouchables* . . . I think he's just now finishing *The Spiral Staircase*. I'll arrange for you to meet him when the time comes."

FREDDY-BABY

"Interesting coincidence," I mused aloud, "Oscar Fraley wrote *The Untouchables* and he's about to publish a new book about Jimmy Hoffa. He and I might partner up to do Frank Sturgis's adventures with Fidel Castro in Cuba."

"Holy crap!" he exclaimed. "Olga said you two were in tight! She also said you and Frank want to do a series of action films. Have you made a deal with him yet?"

"Yessir, and I intend to portray him as an American James Bond, except his actions are based on real things and not fantasy. Another up-side is that Panama could pass for Cuba," I added.

"Who would you see playing Sturgis?" Freddy-Baby asked.

"Charles Bronson would be my first choice," I offered. "I'd try to get his wife, Jill Ireland, too."

"Do you know them?"

"I know their agent, Paul Kohner," I said.

"Do you already have a contract with Sturgis?"

"I'll make you a copy," I smiled. We clinked glasses and did a quick bottoms-up *salut*.

"Morgan, when Olga first mentioned you I was skeptical as hell until you got a thumbs-up from my old man. Whatever you did with him never hit the streets and that says it all. Anyway, welcome aboard."

He poured another round and we toasted–clink-clink–then it went down, too. He smacked his lips and cocked his head before he spoke. "Thanks to Piazza's bullshit, we are *out* in Florida. Now the boss wants me to move Harris & Company to Arizona of all places, where he can keep an eye on them. You'll meet David [Harris] and his partner, Tom Winters, soon enough. They're damned good at acquiring commercial properties and developing them, but they're cocky bastards. Anyway, I'll form a new corporation for us as soon as we get moved to Tucson."

"Why not California?" I asked, curious why sunny and dry Arizona would be a better location than sunny and dry California.

"Let's just say it's what the boss wants," he said with a wink. Olga burst into the room smelling like an advertisement for Coco Chanel.

Fred ushered us into his shiny new Land Rover and we drove south to the posh La Costa Luxury Resort, midway to San Diego. I was not surprised when the maitre d' recognized Kerr and ushered us to a reserved table with a fabulous view.

Indeed, throughout our luncheon, we had visits from characters straight out of "Central Casting for Mafia Hoods." I was backslapped and small-talked by four guys named Tony, two Dominics and one Vito, each impeccably groomed, overly tanned, and heavy with gold everything. The last man to approach jutted one of his chins at Olga to ask if she was yanking his chain about Frank Sturgis and me being buddies. I spoke up for myself, mildly offended that I wasn't asked, and said we were thinking about giving it a try. Olga immediately butted in, assuring him that Frank had told her in person that I held the contract to any books and any movies we might make.

"Yeh? Good fuckin' deal, man. Maybe I can fill in some blanks, know what I mean? I just wished Frankie had blasted that fucking Castro! That bum cost me a fortune," the big man wheezed and then shuffled back to his table.

He was barely out of earshot before Freddy-baby snapped. "Morgan! Don't you ever sell yourself short like that again! That guy and his buddies over there could be one hell of a help to what we want to do. Between them, they must own a couple dozen theaters, for chrissake! You think we came all the way down here for fun?"

"I'm sorry," I apologized, dumbfounded. "I didn't know I was doing that."

"Bull-*shit*," Freddy snapped again. "I've watched you play just a little dumb because most people can't resist filling in blanks," He gave me quite the "you don't fool me" look.

"Don't look at me like that, Morgan! Let's make a deal? Let me groom you and we can make a lot of money, but don't ever play mind-games with our people or they'll shut you out for good."

FREDDY-BABY

When the day ended, I was instructed to tie up my loose ends in Florida and join him in Arizona at my earliest possible convenience.

7
8ONANNO D3COD3D

I rendezvoused with Frank Sturgis in Little Havana within hours of my return to Miami. A man I only knew as "Jake" joined us. I wasn't sure why Frank brought Jake, as he appeared to come only to sit silent throughout my report. I found out later that Jake was Jacob Donald Esterline, a member of the CIA and Frank's control agent throughout his time with Castro. Jake was also the CIA's project director for the Bay of Pigs debacle in Cuba.

After I filled in the blanks, Frank and the previously silent Jake, accepting that I was too far-gone to listen to reason about hanging up my undercover spy routine, took turns providing sketches of the mob's history and current structure.

Their lecture began in the late 1920s when Salvatore Maranzano attempted to organize the American gangster scene by creating what he termed "The Commission." Founding memberships were limited to the heads of New York's "Five Families: himself, Charles "Lucky" Luciano, Joe Profaci, Vincent Mangano, and Tommy Gagliano. They were the leaders of the most powerful crime families in America. Maranzano presumed to assign each boss an equal vote in deciding issues affecting them all while demanding that the majority vote must rule in all disputes.

All went well until 1931 when Maranzano nominated himself to be their *capo di tutti capi*, the "Boss of all the Bosses." That meant that as the odd-numbered member, he held the swing vote in any stalemate. In short, all he had to do was

BONANNO DECODED

buy off two others and he was in total control.

Such arrogance did not set well with Luciano and his under bosses, so they counseled with Meyer Lansky, the grandmaster of criminal psychology. Lansky confirmed their suspicions that Maranzano would plan Lucky's execution so he could replace him with his hand-chosen minions. If Maranzano's plan succeeded, he would become the crime czar to all North America.

Lansky advised Luciano to strike first, suggesting he use the services of Murder, Inc., a group of mostly Jewish and Italian killers who worked for organized crime groups. His choice of hitters: high-profile members Benjamin "Bugsy" Siegel and Samuel "Red" Levine. On September 10, 1931, Bugsy, Red, and others assassinated Maranzano in his office in the Helmsley Building in downtown New York City. With Maranzano dead, his under boss Joseph Bonanno took over his mobster family.

Wisely heeding Lansky's counsel, that same year the remaining heads of the Five Families created a fresh version of Maranzano's "Commission," giving birth to the infamous crime syndicate. This time around, they made an even number of members so that no one could become the "Boss of Bosses" by a simple majority. Moreover, and in recognition of his value both as a financial advisor and a war counselor, Lansky held great influence as their counselor, yet he chose to exercise no vote.

Comparative peace reigned until 1964 when another turf war erupted between the old and the up-and-coming capos. It became so dangerous that Mike Zaffarino, Joe Bonanno's personal enforcer, reportedly kidnapped Joe for his own protection. A full eighteen months passed before Bonanno emerged all tanned and healthy, but he tied the hands of the FBI by refusing to press charges against his supposed kidnapper who happened to be a cousin. Joe took that opportunity to announce to reporters that the strain to his weakening heart was forcing him to retire, and he intended to live out his life in the healing deserts of southern Arizona.

In 1965, Gaspar "Gasparino" DiGregarino took over as head of the Bonanno Family.

"Utter friggin' bullshit," Jake barked and Frank snorted in agreement. In their opinions, Bonanno had used an altered passport, breezing through Canadian Customs at Buffalo to rush to the airport in Montreal. From there he flew to Paris, not London or Rome. After all, Italy would be the first place any FBI tracker might look, and French security paled next to the London's Scotland Yard. However, had Bonanno been traced to France, for all practical purposes, his trail would end there. It was easy to travel incognito anywhere in France by using first-class rail service with private compartments that also provided room service behind drawn curtains.

Moreover, laying down a false trail is easy. One merely purchases tickets to distant destinations but exits at any intermediate stop where one purchases another ticket to wherever. By switching trains often and using zigzag routes, one can enter their true destination quite anonymously.

Jake and Frank also were unanimous in thinking that Bonanno's destination had been Milan, Italy, where he had been an incognito guest at a private villa owned by Roberto Calvi, an up-and-coming officer at Milan's prosperous Banco Ambrosiano, a Catholic bank created to counter-balance Italy's "lay banks. It became known as the "priests' bank." They agreed, too, that shortly after Joe's arrival, an unnamed American-born archbishop from the Vatican commenced making many visits to huddle with Bonanno and Calvi.

Months later, and after the details had been hammered out and their secret deal sealed, the mystery archbishop returned to the Vatican, Calvi returned to his bank where he was awarded a much higher position, and Bonanno slipped back into the United States to emerge from his "captivity."

To celebrate Joe's safe return, Lansky threw a private banquet limited to certain senior bosses. After the usual celebratory speeches and toasts, Meyer confided that he and Bonanno had successfully engineered a money-laundering scheme that could make each of them wealthier than they could ever dream. Better yet, within a few short years they could retire as honest executives with ample incomes generated by legitimate businesses. Ironically, they would pay taxes like any other *shlub* while laughing at the IRS.

How could this miracle come about? Companies they secretly owned through veiled foreign investment groups would retain them as expensive consultants.

BONANNO DECODED

These bold words were too intriguing to ignore; even the most dubious don wanted to hear more.

Meyer prefaced his proposition by reminding them of IRS rules prohibiting the investment of *illegal* profits into *legal* ventures; all such assets were subject to seizure and forfeiture. However, funds imported for investments through *legitimate* offshore agencies were 99.999 percent safe, even from IRS scrutiny. This was especially true if such investors remained minority stockholders in the ventures. This confused his audience. After all, these were men used to command, not tax laws.

Lansky quelled their protests by promising that, should they join him and Joe in providing the first-risk seed-capital to such ventures, legal investors would come running with checkbooks in hand. After all, every venture would be on familiar playing fields like shopping malls, strip malls, commercial buildings, vineyards, California vegetable and fruit truck farms, housing projects and, of course, an independent bank or two. Topping it off, Lansky and Bonanno added their personal guarantees that *any* amount of cash placed in their care would vanish and be untraceable throughout its scrambled route until returning as snow-white capital.

They closed by inviting each capo to join their maiden run for a minimum of $100,000 each. After that, the sky was the limit. Better yet, Bonanno and Lansky guaranteed not a single dime would be lost.

Of course, the aging capos drooled at the potential of morphing from common criminals to respectable executives. Still, they wanted to know how Lansky and Bonanno planned to smuggle cash out and return it as fully laundered monies.

Lansky laid down his iron rule: excepting himself and Bonanno, no one would be privy to that one secret. His logic was that, God forbid, if any one of them was ratted out by some flunky facing life in prison or the gas chamber, who is to say what they might give up to save their neck. That's when Frank Costello, part of the Luciano crime family, angrily pointed out that if Joe and Meyer *alone* held the keys, what would happen to their money if some clown whacked *them*?

Lansky and Bonanno raised their glasses in a toast and Meyer said, "Then it is all your best interests to wish us a long life. *L'chei-im!*"

CITIZEN SPY

The hours of instruction by Frank and Jake ended without further comment. The evening wound down with small talk about the ongoing Cuban situation and the perfidy of the Congress and the White House.

I thanked them for their advice, but commenced wrapping up my business interests in Florida. The worst part would be explaining my move to Emily.

I knew she would be brave . . . until I was out of sight.

A markedly subdued Olga ushered me into her bungalow in Tucson, Arizona. Her report was grim: Fred Kerr's arguments with David Harris had triggered a massive heart attack. Upon release from the hospital, Fred's father transferred him to the small town of Occidental, California. When well enough to return to work, his new assignment was acquiring financial interests for the mob in locally owned banks, commercial vegetable farms, orchards, and vineyards. Nevertheless, Olga assured me that Freddy-baby's dedication to our Panamanian project remained unwavering.

In the interim, Olga insisted that I accept her hospitality until I located a suitable apartment or a condominium and offered to store the file boxes she spied in my rear seat.

I had to ask myself if she was being genuinely hospitable or if she would take inventory while I slept. It didn't matter. I had paused one hundred miles east in the town of Willcox, Arizona, to rent a storage unit. I made sure that anything *too* personal was safe.

Come morning, I waited a full hour after Olga had left for work at the new offices of Harris & Company before reconnoitering my surroundings. I soon discovered a tan-colored thread tautly stretched across the doorway to her bedroom, a scant inch above the matching carpet. I also spied that favorite tape recorder peeking out from a stack of throw pillows nearest the telephone. It was obvious that any conversation not meant for other ears couldn't be had here.

I left searching for the nearest public telephone, antsy to report in to Sturgis. He advised me to return to Olga's and make a fresh call to him so his number would appear on her bill. I should say only encouraging things about working with her while expressing sympathy for Fred, etc.

Once completing that farce, I checked the newspaper for rentals and took a quick tour of Tucson. I dawdled, giving her ample time for her to check her little booby-trap, review her audio tape, and perhaps contact Kerr to make *her* report.

I returned that evening to a candlelight dinner plus some exciting news: Fred had already recruited a prominent attorney out of Houston to act in his stead. In fact, one "Jeff Baker" would be jetting in that weekend to begin laying out our plans. To top off the evening, Olga announced that Butch Piazza, also currently known as New York Metropolitan Correctional Center Inmate Number 36530, would be phoning us from prison that evening, using his once-a-week call privilege

Over dessert, she asked that I do Butch a huge, *huge* favor by flying back to Miami, renting a truck, and hauling Butch's cabin cruiser boat to Arizona. He promised to pay all expenses. However, she emphasized, this mission must be kept secret from everyone except the three of us, and we must not even hint at it over the telephone because guards always listened.

When Butch's call came in, Olga officially introduced me and he cut straight to the chase. Olga, I knew, was listening on another receiver in her room. I was told, not asked, to tell famous crime writer Oscar Fraley that Butch would reveal details that would put a whole load of Florida's top cops and politicians in jail. Moreover, Butch wanted to take a lie detector test to prove every word. In return, Oscar must petition the Feds to set him free through the Witness Protection Program and–oh, yes–he wanted his book to be titled, *The Unwilling Don,* so it might ride on the coattails of Mario Puzo's *The Godfather*. After all, Butch bragged, he was the real deal and not some writer's fantasy.

Next on his little wish list of demands: I must tell Oscar that Butch was forced into a life of crime because he carried the Piazza name, his father and grandfather being true legends in their time. He wanted it known that he had never intended to be a hood; he was better suited to be a film star or maybe a writer. Instead, Butch railed, he was behind bars like a common criminal, and for what? He had only followed orders like a good soldier. After all, would any obedient U.S. Army officer take the heat if his commanding officer screwed up? Hell, no!

CITIZEN SPY

Yet poor old Butch would spend a twenty-year to life sentence in prison.

I worked hard to stay in character, solemnly promising to draft a formal writer's agreement. I would, of course, sign it before sending it to Oscar and then forwarding it to Butch. Then, as Butch's telephone time was ending, I added a stipulation of my own–everything must go through Olga.

The moment we hung up, I knew my demand had worked perfectly. Olga came bounding out of her bedroom, giving me sloppy kisses while her hands explored my back from neck to buns to assure herself that I had no hidden recorder or transmitter. Satisfied that I was clean, she reminded me that her percentage must come out of my end and that Piazza must never know.

Bam! Another bulb flashed in my head, realizing she had struck the same deal with Piazza in order to collect on *both* ends! Clever bitch, this one! Clever criminal, but I had to admire her all the same.

Jeff Baker arrived on schedule. He was a tall, handsome, and affable man with a quick sense of humor. Had I met him poolside, I never would have guessed he was with the mob. Handshakes and smiles over, he cut to the chase. Henceforth he was in charge of the legalities to form our production company and all financing in Panama. Moreover, I was to return with him to Houston to discuss my Sturgis film package with Josef Shaftel, the producer Kerr had previously mentioned. Shaftel was flying in from his London residence for that meeting.

Come Sunday, Jeff and I flew to Houston to rendezvous with Shaftel at Baker's. Negotiations were swift and satisfactory, so we three flew to Los Angeles where we were treated to lunch at the Beverly Hills mansion of Richard Fleischer, director of such film gems as *The Don is Dead, Tora! Tora! Tora!, Barabbas, Mr. Majestyk, Che, The Boston Strangler, 20,000 Leagues Under the Sea, The New Centurions* and *Mandingo*. It was agreed that Fleischer would direct, I would do the script rewrites as he requested, and I also would co-produce with Shaftel. Hands shaken and backs slapped, the deal was ready for Jeff to seal with cash and contracts.

Leaving Shaftel to make his arrangements, Jeff and I jetted back to Tucson to celebrate with Olga. It took no more than two bottles of the bubbly to get Jeff bragging about how our Panamanian productions were to be such a profitable

BONANNO DECODED

charade that "in no time we would in the Big Time."

Once again I followed Frank's advice and joined in by offering a few righteous comments followed by a few deliberately naïve ones until I had Olga and Baker stumbling over themselves to correct me. Shaftel was hired, they said, because he consistently delivered saleable products at minimum costs and squeezed every dime until it bled. Of course, we must pay the American Screen Actors Guild cast and key crewmembers according to their union rules and scale; on the flipside, we would employ every Panamanian in sight because they worked for comparative peanuts. Better yet, Panamanian Dictator Omar Torrijos was offering prison inmate laborers at no cost.

Jeff also bragged that he would make sure that we three would have the sweetest deals of all. To keep our homeland taxes to the minimum, each of us would be paid through two separate accounts. One was under our true names but it would receive a fraction of what was due. The second account would hold the bulk of our money under assumed names, and Torrijos would issue us matching Panamanian passports.

Jeff then drafted Piazza's tell-all agreement for Olga, Oscar Fraley, and me to sign and send to him. He promptly returned a fully executed copy. Only then did I learn that the entire writing deal with Piazza was a deception. Piazza obviously believed he was communicating in confidence with his writers, yet neither Oscar nor I would see a word from him. Someone else acted in our stead, reading every "mob secret" Piazza revealed.

My cooperation bore strange fruit; Olga and I dined at the best tables at five-star restaurants and received their best wine. I was called by my first name by known Mexican Mafia figures who owned the fanciest nightclubs in town, and I could not pick up a check anywhere except Burger King. I had the distinct impression that gangster money owned and operated everything in Tucson

I badly needed a retreat and so, come Christmastime, I flew to Canada to spend the holidays with Emily and my ex-wife's Quebecois family. Despite the joy of seeing Emily, despite the warmth I felt among those wonderful folks whom I had come to love so dearly, something unexpected happened that plunged me into an inner chaos. Emily and her mother had reached an impasse and my beloved child pleaded to come to live with me in Arizona.

I could not refuse.

Emily and I returned to Tucson where we rented a comfortable townhouse. We were happy as clams until Olga decided she wanted to play surrogate mother. She took Emily through every high-dollar mall in town and began inviting herself to our weekend jaunts. I gritted my teeth and tolerated it until Olga began teaching Emily to apply makeup. Panama or no Panama, the time was coming to fold my tent. This wasn't just me anymore, now it involved my daughter. The question was merely when and how.

The following evening Emily and I dodged Olga to attend an Indian handicraft fair in the historic part of Old Tucson on our own. There we encountered an attractive young woman who introduced herself as Doris. If reincarnation is true, we three were related; if not, instant friendship can count as a lovely coincidence.

In our ensuing conversation, Emily and I discovered that she was from the Midwest and, in escaping an over-controlling parent, she had elected to visit a cousin for the summer. However, they, too, had a falling out and she had nowhere to stay. Of course, we invited her to our home where she became more than a welcome guest, she was absorbed into our family.

One day I noticed the scent of marijuana in our home. Poor Doris had no idea why I reacted with such fury; apparently pot and drugs were not only common in her town, one of her school teachers had been among her first suppliers at age ten. This was beyond my ken. We send our children to schools to be taught subjects and values–or so I thought.

By summer's end, I all but forced Doris to return home to complete her studies. Emily and I keenly felt the vacuum she left behind. Later, the same evening that Doris left and when I was sure Emily was asleep, I placed a call to the local DEA office.

Although my intention was only to leave my number for a callback the next day, Agent Norman C.P. Jones took my call. I gave him the most minor of synopses of what I was involved in and was amazed that he agreed to meet me within an hour at Tucson's Smuggler's Inn.

8. THE UNLIKELY TRIO

Norman C. P. Jones:

I was sitting at work. It was a night like every other, when destiny took me by the hand. I answered the phone and fielded Robert Morgan's call. He told me a little of what he claimed to be involved in and I figured he was full of shit. I didn't have anything better on my plate, so I thought I'd pacify the guy and I agreed to meet him that evening at the Smugglers Inn. It was en route to my home and an excuse to have a few beers after a crappy day. In his summation, he mentioned he was involved with filmmaking so I anticipated that any story he had to tell would be 99.9 percent Hollywood bull.

When I got to the Inn, picking out Morgan was like picking out a steak in a freezer full of hamburger. His clean-shaven head, black goatee, and expensive clothing easily set him apart from the relaxed Tucson crowd.

There was little to no small talk between us; it was strictly business. Although he came straight to the point with names, dates, and places, the more he talked the more skeptical I became. In my many years with the DEA, I had never heard of this supposed gangster, John Piazza, nor was I aware of any true Mafia family operating out of Atlanta. The Mafia I knew preferred places like New York or Chicago. Nevertheless, I appeased him by jotting down each name mentioned. Glancing over my list, the only name I recognized was Joe Bonanno–affectionately known as Joey Bananas–but the whole world knew of him, too, so he didn't really count.

CITIZEN SPY

I was so unimpressed with what I considered an obvious yarn that it took nearly a week before I decided to run the names he shared with me.

I had relied on a lot of gut instinct my whole life and I was pretty sure of myself. On this guy, though, I was dead wrong.

Nearly every person he mentioned came up as a serious mobster or a close affiliate, but when I ran a computer check through NADDIS (Narcotics and Dangerous Drugs Information System) on Piazza, he had not one but *three* separate case file numbers. One is enough to put me on high alert, but three screamed, "major crime figure." I ran a check on Morgan, curious about his real motive, and was shocked; he didn't have so much as an outstanding traffic ticket.

I made a quick call, inviting myself to his home within the hour. It was important that I meet him there for two reasons: he would be more comfortable in familiar surroundings and I could gain insight to his lifestyle.

I arrived at Morgan's townhouse, which was clean, neat, and orderly. His furnishings were of quality early Americana style and his walls held limited-edition art prints, one of which was a Salvador Dali. I asked to use his bathroom to see what kind of reading material he generally occupied himself with and noted the magazines were *National Geographic* and *Smithsonian*. Everything about this guy was far from the normal informant. When I returned to the dining room, Robert served a luncheon of soft brie cheese with British water crackers and he offered a choice between Earl Grey tea or espresso.

Nice.

We proceeded to talk for three solid hours while he filled me in on his dual life up to that point. He backed up many of his claims with stacks of hard-copy documentation that he kept intermingled with his script writings as if they were part of his storyline research. Bloody-well brilliant, as the Brits say.

Morgan, not being of the criminal element, was a refreshing change but his status put me in a dilemma. Nearly every informant I had ever worked with was a criminal whose motive to squeal on their partners was for revenge, to save themselves, or to reduce their punishment. That was the usual fare. So our system really had no classification for someone who was doing this dangerous work simply to act as a good Samaritan.

THE UNLIKELY TRIO

Morgan added yet another wrinkle. He agreed to work with me but under *his* rules, not ours. It wasn't often that an informant believed he had the influence to make this kind of request and, under the usual circumstances, I would have laughed and said he needed us more than we needed him. Morgan, though, didn't qualify. We had nothing to hold over him, no potential crime to bust him for, and it put me in a bit of a pickle.

Morgan went on to tell me that he would accept out-of-pocket expenses, but he refused a salary or a reward. I had to work to keep my jaw from gaping open. He reasoned that if he took either a salary or a reward, the DEA would essentially be his employer and could tell him what to do. Moreover, he would take all the suggestions and directions I would offer, but never an order.

I did not return to the office after I left Morgan's house. As a bred-and-born Irishman, I do my best thinking in a pub, so I went back to the Smuggler's Inn for some sequestered time to ponder everything I had learned.

After deciding that I was willing to work with Morgan, I returned to the office and entered his name and all his statistics and information into our system as our newest confidential informant. I chuckled aloud at the irony that Morgan's numerical designation, automatically assigned, was "004." I wondered if this film buff would get a kick out of his double-oh status, a reference to the newly popular James Bond. When I stopped laughing, I tagged my movie guy with the code name "Star."

Fun over, it was time for the real work to begin. In distilling Morgan's information, I realized my agency's earlier suspicions that something big was developing in Arizona were true. The DEA had suspected that the influence of the Mexican Mafia was somehow linked to businesses around Tucson and, while we were aware that former New York Mafia boss Joe Bonanno was living in our midst, we had nothing to tie the two regional crime organizations together . . . until Morgan's allegations. I puzzled over the conundrum of merely using Morgan's information as logical connections when my junior partner, Danny O'Brien, mentioned that he had heard that one Frederick Coward, a top-rated FBI agent with whom he had worked, recently transferred to the FBI's Tucson office to investigate something linked to drug smuggling. Danny assured me that

Coward, like me, was a bit of a renegade who fought the system, pursuing his cases to the bitter end regardless of the consequences. I smiled because I could relate to that. I'd been painted with that brush plenty of times.

Frederick Coward:

As an FBI special agent, I came to Tucson fresh from a two-year undercover operation that had successfully pursued, prosecuted, and convicted members of organized crime in multiple Western states. My fresh assignment was to form a task force to investigate corruption and white-collar crime in Southern Arizona's public sector. At the time, there was no way I could know that DEA Agent Norman Jones and I would soon combine forces with a unique private citizen.

Once settled in with my family, I spent weeks scrutinizing everything that crossed my desk. While much of the illegal activity was the usual payoffs and kickbacks, others hinted at probable links between certain legitimate enterprises and the Mafia for political and financial gain. These types of files piqued my interest.

I was intrigued to discover that several high-profile personalities were involved in serious narcotics trafficking emanating from South and Central America, Mexico, and through the porous southwestern border of the United States. One name popped up too many times to ignore: Joseph Bonanno. I knew Bonanno was the former New York Mafia boss who purportedly moved to Tucson to retire as a "law-abiding citizen." If that were true, why did many of these reports refer to him as a *Godfather* and hint that he somehow controlled every organized criminal activity and enterprise in the southwest, including the narcotics traffic out of South America, Mexico, and the Caribbean?

Bonanno's name drew my attention. He was right there, under my nose, and pretending to be something he wasn't. I wanted to learn more.

Digging deeper, I found it no secret that Bonanno was deemed a close friend to Evo DeConcini, attorney general of Arizona from 1948 to 1949 and a justice on the Arizona Supreme Court from 1949 to 1953. More proverbial lights went on when I discovered that Evo's son, Dennis DeConcini, was now perfectly placed as

THE UNLIKELY TRIO

Pima County Attorney from 1973 to extend to 1976 and was the chief prosecutor and civil attorney for the county and its school districts.

(Dennis DeConcini was elected to the U.S. Senate in 1976 as a Democrat. However, it was later revealed that he was a secret member of the infamous "Keating Five" in a banking and political contribution scandal during the 1980s, which grew out of the U.S. Savings and Loan Crisis. The scandal involved Charles Keating, Lincoln Savings, and its ramifications contributed to DeConcini's early retirement from the U.S. Senate.)

Adding to this curious blend, I noted that Bonanno had frequent yet surreptitious contact with Manuel Sameniego, the gangster and not the artist, who was a known major smuggler of narcotics from Mexico into the United States and Canada.

My problem became finding a way to penetrate Bonanno's organization. Top-level criminals like Bonanno only deal with people whom they have known for *years* and trust. I was puzzling over my dilemma when a random "DEA-6 Report" from the local office came across my desk. Coincidentally, the report contained information and names of people who were also on my list: David Harris, Thomas Winters, Richard Boykin, Olga Elias, Frederick Kerr, and John Charles Piazza III. A quick check revealed that Piazza was already in federal custody and eager to cut a deal.

I grinned. It looked like I had a major Racketeering Influenced Corrupt Organization (RICO) case staring me in the face. Tucson might prove to be a great next step after all. I made a call to the originator of the report, one Norman C. P. Jones, and arranged to meet at his office.

I was surprised to find Jones altogether different than what I had expected; he was not only easy to talk with, we discovered that we each had worked several major cases, had been in shootouts with dopers and gangsters, and also kept a respectable distance from certain fellow agents. On the other hand, my willingness to share all my information impressed him, as that was extremely rare between government agencies, most especially the FBI.

Jones reciprocated by offering to introduce me to his new CI for the case, his very own secret "Star."

Robert W. Morgan:

Norm contacted me to fill me in on the FBI interest and scheduled a meet-and-greet with Fred. Following a brief flurry of grins, handshakes, and toasts, my new handlers tag-team hammered me with a long list of dos and don'ts. Sometimes I felt that all I got from people was a list of dos and don'ts and I wondered if my education on the topic would ever end.

My assignment, as agreed by both Norm and Fred, was to gather raw evidence and report all things seen or heard *without edit* to them. They said I must submit everything in writing and include every detail, no matter how small or meaningless I thought it might be.

I made a single request in return, but it was a request upon which everything hinged. I was willing to do everything they needed and willing to continue to immerse myself in the criminal world I had infiltrated. I was willing to go the distance, no matter what the distance. However, what I required in return was simple: protect my child.

Within one short month, we three had somehow smoothed into a perfectly meshed team. Our association was puzzling to both Norm's and Fred's superiors. It was strange enough for the infamously "haughty" FBI to work closely with the far more "normal" DEA, but to bring in some untrained, inexperienced, and unqualified civilian left many shaking their heads. Indeed, Coward and Jones were constantly justifying my relevance and championing my value, regardless of my amateur status. Regardless, I proved to be an anomaly to their desk-bound, pencil-pushing mentors.

Somehow, we managed to bring out the best in each other: me, the untrained but overzealous normal guy; Norm, the easy-going and amiable cop; and Fred, the focused and determined professional. We accomplished things beyond the dual agencies' usual vision almost daily.

In retrospect, the biggest issue the agencies likely had with me was that they could not control me. I could walk away in a heartbeat and, if I so chose, no one could force me to testify to what I learned, saw, or heard because they had no leverage.

Their doubts or worries were really quite unfounded, though. All three of us knew that to accomplish our objectives, Jones and Coward must dodge, bend, or sometimes ignore certain bureaucratic regulations and I must stay the course regardless. Moreover, since they could not share certain facts with me because everything on their end was confidential, I had no true clue how far-reaching our deal could and would become; that is, until several years later.

One of my initial assignments was gathering and reporting contact information that Olga maintained. I did as asked and compiled an extensive list from her personal telephone Rolodex. The information I provided to Norm and Fred was recorded and later helped another infamous case of international espionage come into better focus. Apparently, one number belonged to the Metropolitan Jail in San Diego, California, where Daulton Lee and Christopher Boyce of *The Falcon and the Snowman* infamy were confined. Lee and Boyce were two young Californian men from wealthy families, convicted of selling U.S. security secrets to the Soviet Union in the 1970s.

Yes, indeed, Bonanno's operation had far-reaching tentacles.

Undercover life wasn't always a bed of roses. In 1979, Olga had one of her regular phone conversations with Piazza and he told her that he was sure there was a mole in her midst. Apparently, he had seen a document that stated, among other things, plans to pull her phone records, vest designs meant to smuggle money out of the country, information about her dealings with a man named Hector Rodriguez. Olga confided in me that she though either her house was bugged or an associate named Cathy had spoken out of turn.

While I maintained a nonchalant attitude, I was sweating bullets. I knew that suspicion could easily lead to me as I had been one of only three people, including Olga, who knew about the money-smuggling vest design.

It was during this conversation that Olga dropped a bomb on me, though I tried to keep things in perspective. I had really enjoyed the thought of getting the full Piazza story directly from the man himself, then making a film based on him.

I knew, deep down, that it wasn't *really* something viable—I was working against him for goodness sake. However, I can't say it didn't sting a little when Olga advised me that Piazza, who wasn't as trusting, had decided he no longer wanted to continue his contract with me.

My report to Norm was scathing. I told him everything I had been told and finished my report by indicating that, while I was working for nothing other than "doing the right thing" and acting in good faith, someone in either his or Fred's office was not. I continued by telling him that my ability to continue as an intelligence source had been sorely damaged.

However, as usual, I followed my orders until things smoothed over.

Back in my Mafia life, I had wrung Olga dry of new information and she affirmed that our film studio deal was still on ice. I found an excuse to remove Emily from Tucson, sending her to the tiny, remote ski-resort town of Whitefish, Montana. There, at least, my baby was away from Olga's influence and attending school with wonderfully clean-cut kids with a yen for the out-of-doors.

Once settled in, and at my handlers' direction, I reconnected with Fred Kerr, aka "Freddy-baby," in Northern California. Of course, I told Jones and Coward about the reconnection. Both were excited when Fred invited me to visit his hideaway ranch in Occidental to meet Hedy, his new Lebanese wife. After all, while Fred was a prime target, his wife was also a known dealer in illegal arms to warring nations in the Middle East.

As planned, Coward and Jones rendezvoused with me in San Francisco in a parking garage adjacent to Kerr's office at One Lombard Street. However, while rigging my concealed microphone and tape recorder, the best technology of the day, they discovered they were missing the customary roll of surgical tape used to attach the microphone and its cord to my chest. My consummate pals didn't hesitate: Coward reached into his official FBI handy-dandy, all-purpose tool kit for a strip of super-stick, commercial-grade, could-strap-a-dump–truck-to-a-building-strength duct tape and pasted everything against my bare skin. While Fred taped me up, maybe even using more of that duct tape than necessary, Jones slit the inner seam on my brand-new, barely out-of-the-box cowboy boots to insert the recorder.

THE UNLIKELY TRIO

They sent me on my way with a laundry list of things to keep an eye out for surrounding Freddy-baby.

After completing my reunion with Kerr and managing to record all the answers to the assigned questions, I went to return the tape recorder to my keepers, who moved swiftly to recover their equipment. All went well until they realized their microphone was damn well stuck beneath the super-sticky duct tape!

There was no avoiding it. If I was to return the equipment, it was going to cost me dearly and my payment was in flesh. Hiding smirks, the two agents pretended to feel remorse as they forcibly recovered their equipment. As for me, it took more than a month for my damned skin to grow back.

That evening, as the Kerrs and I prepared to leave for a fine dinner and a casual trip north along the scenic Pacific Coast Highway, Fred slipped something into my pocket. It was a magnificent and ornate ring holding a huge emerald encircled with diamonds. My visit, it seemed, coincided with their first wedding anniversary. Freddy asked me to produce his twenty-thousand dollar gift for his wife after dinner when he planned to kneel in front of her for a second time to thank her for their wonderful first year.

Part of me wanted to slap him on the back for the romantic and loving gesture of love. The realist in me remembered, however, that the money used to fund the purchase of the amazing gem originated from kids who spent their lunch money on his damned addictive and life-altering drugs. That enabled the pudgy son of a bitch to play Don Juan to an arms-dealing bitch who further profited by selling arms and ammunitions meant only to mangle, maim, and slaughter human beings.

Not nearly as romantic and sweet when you keep it in perspective.

That weekend was the first in a series of visits over the summer, enabling me to discover, uncover, photograph, and record a plethora of incriminating data.

One night, an extraordinarily heavy rainstorm struck and his guesthouse flooded. Fred apologized profusely and decided it was only proper to put me up in his office, out of the sopping mess. As fate would have it, it was the same room where he was in the middle of preparing his income taxes. What a wondrous mess I suddenly was immersed in: files and records strewn everywhere, and cabinets open and unlocked.

I burned through every roll of film I had for my Minox camera while learning that he was helping invest millions of dollars, mostly for Caribbean-based clients, into every bank, vineyard, and vegetable truck farm in sight.

The following day, I had yet another bit of serendipitous luck. The Kerr's sole neighbor, one Frederick Drykerman of San Diego, popped in to exchange a few words with Hedy. Normally I would pay scant attention to such exchanges, but this sour-faced man not only ignored my introduction, he appeared to rush away, scurrying back through their connecting gate. His actions made me suspicious. Later that day, I took a casual stroll through the forest of huge redwood trees bordering Fred's property. All seemed ordinary enough until I ambled along unneighborly "Mister McNasty's" fence.

He had a rather nice yet unremarkable home set back in a grove of redwoods. All looked normal until I spied a long cable running up the trunk of his tallest tree. Following it up with my eyes, I made out a cleverly concealed ham-radio antenna spread amidst its limbs. I won't say that I did an "ah-ah, I gotcha," but it crossed my mind. After all, up to now, I had no idea who that neighbor was nor had I questioned his right to have a shortwave antenna in his tree. Nevertheless, Frank Sturgis had taught me that, when acting as an undercover operative, one must never overlook nor prejudge any unusual act, word, gesture, or fact as each could be a random piece to an unexpected puzzle.

Sturgis had been correct. The CIA exploded when Coward and Jones circulated my report; we had apparently just solved a long-standing mystery. The antenna I reported seeing was used to broadcast stolen, secret American defense information to pro-Communist factions in Central and South America. However, they did this at unpredictable times and always in such quick bursts that the U.S. Air Force signal-seekers and aerial observations had been unable to pinpoint the point of origin because of the damned tree.

Things at the Kerr ranch changed markedly on my next visit. My old, friendly Freddy-baby was stiff and withdrawn and our conversation was stilted. Moreover, it was totally out of character when he insisted we take a ride up the coast to visit old Fort Ross, the former Russian trading post that borders a deserted stretch of

THE UNLIKELY TRIO

highway. This was too odd for me to grasp. It wasn't a pleasant day and Fred was not prone to sightseeing.

Still, to refuse such a request would send the wrong signal, a signal that might say I was afraid to be alone with him.

Comforted to some degree knowing Coward and Jones would (probably) be close behind us, I agreed to his jaunt. For the first and only time, I ignored our rules and plucked Maggie May from her hiding place in my VW while retrieving my sunglasses. I knew this was totally against the law and, if I had to take him down, no one–including my handlers–could save me from the world of hurt that would be waiting.

Kerr took me on what felt like the longest ride of my life. The tense air was thick, dark, and palpable. Nevertheless, I chattered about this, that, and a whole bunch of nothing, trying to make everything seem normal until we reached our destination.

I thought to myself that it was a lousy day to die. The sky was overcast, the ocean was a matching gray, the wind was biting and cold. The parking lot near Fort Ross was empty, and even the damned gates were locked. Fred stammered some excuse about needing to use the only outdoor public telephone and left me standing outside his Land Rover. The hill across the way was empty, rocky, and full of dense, overgrown brush. My already too-tense mind was working overtime, saying what a perfect place the hill was for a sniper. I moved to the far side of the car, waiting for Fred to come back.

When he returned, he had apparently decided the trip was over and we got right back into the vehicle. The return drive seemed interminable, and I managed to make up an excuse to leave the next day for Whitefish, Montana. The usually affable Kerr offered no comment, no objection, nor did he ask me to stay another day.

Instead of going to Whitefish, Emily and I once again returned to Tucson where I wrote out my eleven-page report. Frankly, I was damned proud of my report. I knew I was delivering solid gold information.

My elation, however, was short-lived. When Jones and Coward arrived at my home to collect my work, they resembled twin grim reapers on official business. After accepting my material without comment, my handlers told me that the entire operation had been shut down. My jaw dropped. I was "officially reminded" of my confidentiality agreement and advised, too, that they would no longer be responsible for my well-being nor for that of my Emily's. I was on my own, despite having put my life on the line for what I had assumed was a just cause.

To say that I was stunned speechless is an understatement and the term "stone-cold" took on new meaning. My handlers' parting comments were that both the FBI and DEA had been ordered–emphasis on the word *ordered*–to immediately shut down the current investigation, let loose all involved parties, and seal and forward *all* records to the respective headquarters in Washington, DC.

As reward for a "job well done," the FBI offered Coward his choice of any duty station in the world.

The seemingly far less-grateful DEA simply put Jones back on the streets, assigning him to the border to arrest punks.

Norman Jones:

Several times during my career, I have been ordered to close down an important and intense investigation right in the middle. No reasons are given and I usually am led to believe that the State Department or the CIA is involved. The implication being that the inquiry either is getting dangerously close to national interests or possibly a covert operation.

I had noticed for some time that the special agent in charge of the DEA office in Tucson continually derided my joint case with the FBI and our unwritten adversary, claiming we were spending too much money with little results, among other issues. At first, I believed this was because he couldn't understand the magnitude of the big picture and his desire to settle back into a safe and secure retirement environment.

Upon receiving these orders, I explained to Special Agent in Charge Eyman the implications of what Special Agent Coward and I had uncovered and the different directions being investigated. The orders were reinforced. Valuable

THE UNLIKELY TRIO

information was coming in, so I continued working on the case on the side.

Several days later, I again was called into the SAIC's office and told that if I did anything further on this case, I would be fired. I later was led to believe that the whole real estate market in Tucson and elsewhere was in jeopardy. Subsequently, I was transferred, "for my career development," to Detroit where I successfully worked undercover with the Mafia.

One of the saddest days of my life came when I met with Bob in his home and had to tell him the news. I had no reason to give, no explanation, because it didn't make any sense to me either. I was especially aware that Star we were hanging him out to dry and giving him no protection despite all the dangerous and difficult assignments he had successfully accomplished.

I felt ashamed of and for my bureau.

Years later, Bob and I reconnected and we are still in touch. It is extremely rare for an agent to have any contact with a former confidential informant. Bob, however, isn't just an informant . . . he is now a friend.

9 FROM MOSCOW TO EAST END
REVELATIONS

In truth, I felt abandoned, lost, wrung out, and lonely. Was I being ordered to quit, too? What was the point of me continuing if the whole reason for this mission—having the upper echelon exposed and held accountable for their actions by doing federal time—was stripped from me?

I immediately set a course to distance myself from the mob. It took time, but I was disposable for once and not considered a threat. It was doable.

I tried returning to a normal life. I went from one boring post to another. I finally understood what folks meant when they said they were depressed. The film life, and my company, had gone in another direction when I left Florida and broke all my ties. The sole light in my life was my daughter, but by now, she was grown up and living the busy life of a college student.

Thankfully, the Gods took pity on me and I received a phone call from an old acquaintance in the film business. He was in a partnership to be the executive producer for the first co-production between the United States and the USSR under the new *perestroika*, or "openness," policy of Mikhail Gorbachev. My friend admitted he was in way over his head and asked if I would be interested in visiting Moscow with him. He would put me in charge of creating the storyline, writing the screenplay, and directing.

Of course, Old Fort Ross, being Russian in historic reference, leaped to mind. I did some fast research, wrote what I could, and left for Moscow. The storyline

FROM MOSCOW TO EAST END REVELATIONS

I had written went over extremely well and the Russians loved it. Because of this initial success, I was invited to take part in the 1989-'90 "Save the Children" tour along with a host of public figures and entertainers. As dinner was being served one evening, I was unexpectedly shuttled off to a far corner while my executive producer pal was drawn into conversation with his Soviet counterparts at Paritet Studios. The problem, it seemed, was he had produced only one feature before this, and he had gotten this velvet gig through his father's connections in Washington DC. His inexperience became evident when, each time the professionals involved in the film asked a technical question, he would find a reason to trot to my table. These men were no idiots; they realized I was supplying the answers. It didn't take long before they invited me to join them.

We discussed, at length, which talent we were expecting. I also told the group that I was recruiting my line producers out of Los Angeles, Tom Spalding and his wife Sally Roddy.

Tom, Sally, and I had completed our second visit to Moscow and were returning to Los Angeles via London where they needed to pause to arrange a bit of technical, post-production assistance at Pinewood Studios. I had begged off accompanying them. I thought they deserved time alone. For that matter, so did I. The three of us had been solving problems twenty-four/seven for the past month. Besides, I was hell bent on rewarding myself with a black Burberry trench coat from Harrods, London's famous department store. Lucky for me, it was only blocks from our hotel and I welcomed the stroll.

I had waited curbside with the Spaldings until the Pinewood limousine came to fetch them and was waving goodbye when I heard someone gasp behind me.

"*Morgan?!*"

I turned.

Did I offer my hand first, or had Fred Kerr? I don't recall, nor can I say who broke the silence amid our shuffling feet and shifting eyes. Freddy-baby, of all people, somehow stumbled across me in London. Of course, we both lied and said the other looked great. I was quick to add that I was only passing through with my producers. I told Fred that we were planning a feature film in Russia and my friends had just pulled away.

He asked if the limousine had tinted windows and I (truly) had not noticed. I had no idea he was in London or why, and told him as much. We exchanged business cards as if to confirm the mutual legitimacy of our stories. His read: "Victoria House, #51, Southampton Row, London, telephone 71-405-0040."

I watched his lips moving while he read mine.

"So if you're doing something in Russia, why are you here?" he asked.

"We're checking on some special post-production facilities at Pinewood. Moscow's still a bit shy on the technical side, but I'm confident they'll catch up."

"Why you didn't you go?" he pressed, eyebrow raised in curiosity.

"I'm not all that involved with those details," I said. "Besides, we've been joined at the hip for the past month and I think we all needed the break."

Fred shot a fast glance at his wristwatch. "I'm late for a meeting that I can't miss. Let's have a few drinks tomorrow and catch up with things."

"I'd love to, bud," I said, "but it will have to wait until the next time. We're catching an early flight."

"Yeah, sure," Fred sniffed.

I thought it polite to inquire about Hedy and was surprised when he spat on the sidewalk and twisted his shoe in it. "Screw that bitch! She flipped on me when things got hot and freakin' near put me away for good."

"Sorry..." was all I could offer. I had no idea what happened after I was taken off the case.

My mind was doing back-flips over the bizarre coincidence of running into Kerr so far from our previous stomping grounds. No one on earth knew Tom, Sally, and I intended to stay a night or two while passing through London. Moreover, we had no idea where we would roost until we contacted the studio and *they* had made our reservations under the Spaldings' name, not mine.

Like it or not, my encounter with Fred was wholly and honestly serendipitous.

When our conversation fell into comparing London's weather to Northern

FROM MOSCOW TO EAST END REVELATIONS

California's, we both knew it was time to regroup. Still, Fred did not let go easily; he changed his invitation, asking me to join him for dinner that evening. The request came across as more of a challenge than an invitation.

To make matters worse, he insisted on sending a taxicab so we could dine at his favorite Chinese restaurant in London's East End. I felt a phantom fist slam into my gut. Even I knew there were areas in East London that could be as dangerous as New York's Harlem, especially at night.

"Freddy, m'man, you gotta be kidding," I laughed. "I was looking forward to shepherd's pie, bangers and mash, Sunday roast with Yorkshire pudding, or maybe just good old fish and chips with a pint or two."

"No, no, you owe me this favor," he argued. "See, my new wife is Chinese and her family owns it [the restaurant]; you'd be honoring them. Besides, she's never met any of my American friends."

Was he testing me? Before I could conjure a reasonable excuse, I heard my macho side promising to be waiting curbside at 7 p.m. sharp.

Our parting hug was quick and phony. It was obvious that we each wanted to put time and space between us to think and wonder and plan.

He stood watching while I re-entered my hotel.

I waited a full ten minutes before I slipped out through the hotel's service entrance to trot in the opposite direction. I doubled back twice to see if he might be ghosting me. Seeing nothing of him, I hurried to Harrods. Without even realizing it, I found myself walking straight through the store and out the other side. I chided myself on how ridiculous I was acting. Kerr already knew where I was staying and he had a fifty-fifty shot that I would show up that evening, so why would he care if I did a little shopping?

Besides, I thought, if this night would prove to be my last, I was determined to go out wearing my very own Burberry!

Purchase made, I rushed back to my room to record on the gorgeous hotel stationary every word Kerr and I had exchanged. I addressed the envelope to Jones and Coward, in care of Jones, back in the States and tucked Fred's business card inside. I attached a note to the front for the Spaldings, asking them to mail the letter should I *maybe* come up missing before slipping it under their door.

Despite a long, hot bath, a soft bed, and a movie on the "telly," my mind refused to shut down. When the appointed hour was nigh, I dressed and slipped twin business and hotel cards inside each of my socks. Call me paranoid, but should someone find my body floating down the Thames River sans shoes, perhaps they would give a clue to my identity.

On the appointed hour, one of those signature black London cabs slid curbside outside my hotel. It was the first time I'd noticed how much they resembled miniature hearses.

"Oi! Mister Morgan, is it?" the bony driver called around his dangling cigarette. "Come along, guv, we 'ave quite the drive."

It was indeed "quite the drive," and the further we drew away from central London, the dimmer and more rundown the neighborhoods became.

"Excuse me, sir," the cabbie said after checking his clipboard. "D'ya mind me askin' what takes a gent like you to these parts this time of night?"

"I've been invited to dinner with someone I'd known in the States," I offered.

The cabbie glanced at the address. "He's a Chink, is he? He didn't sound like it when he called or me wife would've told him I was booked up. Never know nowadays. I liked it better when England was for the English, no offense, sir."

"None taken," I smiled. "In fact, I agree with you. Anyway, he's American but his new wife's Chinese. Why do you ask?"

"Well, guv, most parts of East London can be just fine. I've lived here all me life, I have. Bred and born right close to the Bow Bells, if you take me meaning."

"You're a true Cockney then," I said.

"Good on you to know that, mate! However, where you're going," he offered, stressing the *you're*, "can get a bit dodgy. You'll want to keep that fine coat in hand. That cost a pretty pound, I'd say. Could get rough if they take a fancy to it."

"I'm a bit overdressed, ey?" I asked with a grin.

He barked a laugh and shot me a wink as we turned down a grimy side street that burrowed down a canyon of sad and shoddy tenements where bare light bulbs

FROM MOSCOW TO EAST END REVELATIONS

dangled from peeling ceilings.

"If you're wearing a jockstrap, and I'm not meaning to be personal, it'd be a good place to stuff your watch and wallet," he offered.

My gut wanted to spasm. Me and my big mouth, damn it. Was I being stupid, agreeing to meet Kerr's challenge? Should I be smart, fold my wings, return to my clean, neat, and orderly hotel, accept no calls or visitors, and exit England in the morning without another word?

I knew I couldn't, even if it was the smarter thing to do. What I had done to him and his kind, if what I had done had even really amounted to anything, had been right as rain. Try to sell dope or be an eager participant in an organization that sells dope to my kid, your kid, or any kid and you'll have me as an enemy for life. Besides, Freddy-baby had stuttered, not me.

Still, I had no concept how that evening's revelations would affect me for the rest of my life.

The cab slid to a halt before a crumbling brick building midway down the dingiest block I had seen yet. Worse, the restaurant was on the second floor, above a shuttered food market fronted by grimy plate-glass windows. The sole access was up a flight of rusty stairs bolted to the outside wall. Above the entrance, a neon sign dimly blinked "Chinese Food" in English and Chinese logograms. The "welcome" sign seemed prophetic rather than inviting; only the second syllable worked.

I sat staring as it beckoned "come-come-come" until my driver's voice broke my somber reverie.

"I'll wait a bit, mate, if you don't mind. Ten minutes should do to scout it out, yeh? And I'll keep me motor running and my tire iron handy should you change your mind." He smiled, reassuringly.

I handed him my business card and paid triple his fare plus a fifty-dollar tip in exchange for his promise to return at exactly 11 p.m. If I did not appear, he was to fetch Scotland Yard. I asked, too, if he would stash my Burberry in the boot of his cab. If I disappeared, he should wear it in good health.

"Aw, we'll both be here, guv'nor. You can count on that," he said with a wink and a grin. "By the way, me name is Jaime, and I'm pleased to meet you."

CITIZEN SPY

Upon reaching the top landing, I exchanged finger-wriggles with Jaime before pushing inside. I immediately was swallowed in a thick haze of cigarette smoke, and the stench of hot oil, seared onions, garlic, ginger, and more spices than I knew existed hung heavily in the air. As if drawn by a common string, the scattered patrons swiveled around to stare my way. I stood, debating retreat, when Freddy-baby sprang up from a distant corner to wave me in his direction. He alternated between surprise and delight while introducing me to the neatly dressed Oriental woman seated beside him.

"I didn't really expect . . . Bobby, this is my wife, Shu-lee."

"*Nee*-how-mah," I said, in my best Chinese.

"*Nee*-how!" Shu-lee smiled. "Oh, you speak Chinese? My Freddy, you no tell me!"

"Don't let me fool you, ma'am; that's all I remember," I grinned back.

"Oh, but you say so right! Where you learn?" she asked, seeming genuinely curious.

"I picked up a few words at the Lutheran Mission in Kowloon; I was confirmed there when I was in the Navy."

"You sit, please?" she smiled, covering her mouth in the manner of polite Orientals. I hadn't sat for more than a few seconds before a parade of exotic dishes commenced in perfectly timed succession.

I was pleasantly surprised. Despite the shabby surroundings, it was excellent cuisine prepared in the Shandong style, my favorite because it was the least greasy of the usual selections. The only items I fully recognized were the sweet-and-sour yellow river carp and the swallow's nest soup that ended our feast. I was thankful, too, that our conversation was light and easy.

When the last dish cleared, Shu-Lee excused herself to join an elderly Chinese couple seated at a table near the door.

I had a predetermined storyline to fit the "me" he used to know and started barking it out before Freddy-baby could draw his breath.

"Listen up, man! It's good to see you and all that, but I want some friggin' answers. The crap really hit the fan when I got back to Tucson after my last visit to your ranch in Occidental. My townhouse got broken into and so did my filing

FROM MOSCOW TO EAST END REVELATIONS

cabinets. The next day began a string of nasty-ass visits from the FBI *and* the DEA! They fried my tush for hours, man. Hours! Even the local fuzz jumped on me! I couldn't drive ten blocks to get a six-pack without being pulled over five times!"

"Y-you could have called," Freddy stuttered.

"Call who?" I glared, "*You?* I wouldn't have sent you so much as a freakin' smoke signal! Check this out: somehow, the Feds got a copy of my book contract with Piazza. What was I supposed to do, deny it?"

"What did you tell them?"

"What's to tell?" I ranted, sitting back a little in my chair. "I'd only talked with that son of a bitch a few times and all I got were empty promises and lots of bragging bullshit!"

"Yeah, well, he ratted everybody out to the Feds so he could get out on the Witness Protection Program. Then he screwed that up so now he's back in [jail] for good," Fred offered, quickly glancing around. "I heard he's so scared he has to take his showers alone. Sooner or later, he'll get offed and some con's family will get a big present. He's a walking dead man, understand?"

I understood.

"I don't *want* to know and I don't give diddly-shit about him," I shot back. "But I gotta ask you man-to-man, Fred: did you fink me out?"

"What the *hell*," he sputtered, glaring and clutching the edge of the table. "*I* took the heat, not you!"

"Wanna bet?" I bellowed, pointing my finger smack between his eyes. "The Feds were about to charge me with destroying evidence relevant to a federal investigation, for chrissake! Outside of you, Olga, Coco, and your father, who the hell else knew I'd helped Mikey Ducks take those bags of files down to that boat in The Grove?"

"How the hell would I know?" he countered.

"OK, so who else besides you and Olga knew I'd taken Ducks to see my movie when his 'Wanted' poster was plastered around every post office in town? The FBI even had pictures of me having dinner with her [Olga] and Jeff Baker at the Arizona Inn. Want to know who was at the next table? *Joe Bonanno*," I sneered, "the friggin' Boss of Bosses, that's who!"

"Yes, b-b-but . . . "

"B-b-but, my ass," I fired back. "They even knew two of Bonanno's boys had followed me into the men's room as if we were doing some monkey business."

"Oh . . . were you?" he asked, curious.

"All I did was take a leak, but the fact that I was alone with them painted a federal bull's-eye on my skinny ass! They wrung me out like a dishrag, man. So now I got to ask you face-to-face: was the rat-fink Mikey, Baker, Olga, or *you*?"

"Everyone said it had to be you!" he blurted.

"Oh, right on, man! Blame the freakin' new dude who'd never made a single dime with you guys. Know what's worse? I got blackballed! I haven't sold a single script since all that shit went down. I paid one hell of a price for even *knowing* you and that jerk-off Piazza!" I uttered, disgusted.

"I'd heard you got to be some sort of a honcho with the Arizona prison system," Fred snapped back. "Was that your pay-off?"

"Oh, for chrissake! Why would I risk my life messing with Lansky and the Bonannos for some chump-ass go-fer job taking orders from a mental-midget bureaucrat who thought he knew everything but didn't?"

"So how did you get that job?" he pressed.

"Hell, I'd been all over Europe for months doing some artsy-fartsy research for Haseko Komoten Corporation out of Tokyo. While I was gone, my girl, Toni, got in as executive secretary to Larry Hecker, the chief of staff for Governor Babbitt. When I got back, I had to help put bread on the table so she put in a good word."

"What position was that?" he asked.

"I got on with ARCOR," I replied. Seeing his blank look, I continued. "Arizona Correctional Enterprises. It was part of the Arizona prison system that put inmates to work. I made a bunch of sweetheart deals with private-sector employers to pay trustees minimum wage, but they had to guarantee them a real job once they'd earned parole.

"Inside the walls, I had inmates assembling office furniture, hand-crafting wooden toys, and hobbyhorses for day-care centers, and producing structural

FROM MOSCOW TO EAST END REVELATIONS

steel for public projects. Some of the women made airline reservations. Want to check me out? Call my old boss, Tom Lescault. He's still hooting around Phoenix somewhere."

Fred's eyes blinked like a stop light. "How was I to know all that?"

"Yeah, well, use some of your big-time contacts in Phoenix; I'm sure you still have them. Oh," I continued nonchalantly, "by the way, I did try to call you after the heat died down, but you'd vanished."

Fred raised and waggled twin double-shot glasses overhead until Shu-Lee trotted over with a fresh bottle of Dewar's Signature Scotch Whisky. She ignored my offer to pay; instead, padding back to resume her watch-and-wait vigil while he poured hefty shots. We clinked rims and downed our poisons straight and neat.

"OK, Bobby," he choked, "here's what went down after I last saw you. Hedy got nailed for selling her boom-boom crap to the Palestinians. She had to give me up to save herself. All she got was her pockets picked and a slap on the wrist. Me? I got the *permanent* shaft."

"Don't tell me you served time!"

"No, yes . . . well, sort of," he admitted. "The Feds knew I'd never survive jail with my bad heart, so they wrung me dry before kicking my ass out of the country. I'd get serious time if I so much as set one foot back on American soil."

"Sorry, Fred, I didn't know. At least you landed on your feet and you're still as dapper as ever. Where's your tailor–Seville Row or Chelsea?"

"Yeah, right," he snorted. "Now I'm putting piss-ant deals together to scrape by. But listen, what I can't handle is not being allowed to see my kid. That bitch Jill won't let him come here so I'll never get to be with him until he's grown up. It's tearing me up inside, man! I really love him and I'd always planned to be a big part of his life just like what you had with your daughter, you know?

"Now I'm stuck in a second-class Chink restaurant in a shit part of town making penny-deals for idiots! I used to have class, man; I used to be respected, remember?" he whined.

"Oh, I remember everything," I said and took a turn pouring drinks. We downed not one, not two, but three quick rounds. I needed to scald my throat until my eyes watered; I needed serious pain to keep from strangling this whining son of a bitch. Then, when I knew he was taking his last gasp on earth I'd send him off with my fervent hope that some burned-out scum-ball numb-nut bastard was peddling pot, crystal meth, crack cocaine, or pure heroin at *his* kid's schoolyard. Why would any sane person do that to a child? Because, just like Fred, they wanted tailor-made clothes, a bigger BMW, or another emerald-and-diamond ring.

I reminded myself to keep it cool and get a grip on my emotions. I had to regain my calm, detached, and objective persona. Besides, I wondered what more might I wring out of this wimp. Knowledge is power and power allows us to choose to help a friend or destroy an enemy, but it won't permit us to aimlessly float through life. Once again, I felt like a protective shepherd drawing a bead on some lamb-killing coyote.

"Hey, it's hard to believe Hedy ratted you out," I said with a faked sigh. "You two were such a magical team."

"That's what I thought," he said, pouring another round. "So tell me about Russia and all the broads you banged."

"Me? I'm still a virgin," I grinned. "Ever hear from any of the old gang?"

"Let's change the subject."

"OK, but is there anything I can do for you when I get back to the States?" I asked, wondering why he was being so obstinate.

"No."

"Well, I hope you get hooked up with some goodfellas over here and make some coins again," I offered.

"Either talk about something else or let's call it an evening," he snapped.

I sprang to my feet so fast my chair slid back and bounced off the wall. I shot Shu-lee a glare that froze her still as stone while her tablemates scurried for the kitchen.

"Sit down, for chrissake," Fred hissed.

"You think I'm wired, right?" I demanded.

"It's not that–" he stammered.

"Either you pat me down, you son of a bitch, or I'm walking out and you'll wonder for the rest of your miserable life if I'd been a snitch or not. Take your choice, Freddy-baby," I said while rounding the table.

FROM MOSCOW TO EAST END REVELATIONS

I made a slow 360-degree turn to offer every possible nook, tuck, and cranny where a wire or a recorder potentially could be concealed. Once he was satisfied I was clean, I yanked him to his feet and took a turn. To add insult to injury, I made a production of swiping my hands beneath the table and each chair. Finding nothing, I raised my glass.

"*Lekhayim! Shalom alaichem*," I said, offering a cheer.

"*Alaichem shalom*," he grunted, finishing off his drink too quickly. I slipped my glass beneath the table's rim to dribble between my feet while he coughed and sputtered.

"OK, Fred, now that we're off that merry-go-round, let's fill in some blanks. What made you think I was a snitch?"

"Everyone thought so," he admitted.

"I thought we were friends." I said.

"Me, too, but during discovery my attorney said the FBI had those pictures you'd taken of us shooting that special shotgun of yours. They even had one of you riding my horse. How'd they get those except from you?"

"Oh, for chrissake, man! I have copies at my house but I'd sent some up to your ranch in Occidental, too. You know, to thank you for such good times and . . ." I purposefully trailed off. "Whoa, wait up. Didn't I see Hedy always picking up the mail? And didn't you just say she'd flipped on you?"

"Well, yeah, but she said . . ." he drifted off. I could see the wheel in his brain spinning as he began to think. "*A*wwww, *shit!* So *that's* why she kept stirring the pot against you!"

I furrowed my brows. "In all that 'discovery' crap, did you see anything about Butch's personal weapons?"

"No. Why?"

"Had I been a snitch, you'd have seen something about his two fancy handguns, his sniper rifle, a .45 Thompson submachine gun, and a portable printing press."

"What did they have to do with you?" he questioned.

"Olga gave them to me to ditch," I admitted.

His eyes bulged and his lips pooched in and out like a fish out of water, gasping for air. "Wait, wait. When did that go down?"

"Right after Butch got busted," I said. "She told me to get rid of everything."

"*Jesus-Christ-son-of-a-bitch!* Where?" he pressed.

"A place called Chokoloskee. It's a fishing village on the west side of the Everglades."

"Why there?"

"Because it has mosquitoes up the ying-yang that time of night," I explained, "and nobody in their right mind would be outside nosing around except a goofball like me. Look, don't worry. I used the longest dock I could find and pitched everything into the lagoon. It's not pure salt water but it'll rust everything up pretty good."

"Not our press!" he whined.

"Relax. Even if some fisherman snags it, he'd never guess what it is. Hell, I didn't even know what it was," I laughed.

Fred's face blanched white and he shook his head in disbelief. "You threw our plates into salt water?"

"Plates? You mean dishes?" I asked, being intentionally dimwitted.

"No-no-*no!* Our *printing* plates! They were on the press!" Fred's face went from white to red. He was livid.

"Didn't see any . . ." I said, looking up and right to mimic thinking. "Oh, wait. I knocked over a package in the trunk of Olga's rental and it sort of clunked."

"Then you saw them?"

"I didn't see what was inside. She had it wrapped in plastic and duct tape. I can't tell you what was actually in it." I was being honest.

"How big was the package?" he pressed. "Show me or tell me!"

"I'd guess maybe six by four by maybe eight inches," I said, using my hands to approximate the dimensions.

"I swear Bobby, this could be more important than you could dream! Did Olga say exactly where she was going?" He seemed to be suddenly panicking, desperate for the information.

"She said was in a hell of a rush to get to Butch's boat, wherever that was."

FROM MOSCOW TO EAST END REVELATIONS

"She lied to us!" he almost shouted, pounding his fist on the table hard enough that the shot glasses leaped in the air. "That bitch kept them for herself! Oh, she is so dead, dead, *dead*! Wait, wait, Morgan! Did she ever mention that boat again?"

I paused, pretending to think it over. "Maybe once, just after I'd moved to Tucson. She wanted me to go back to Miami to haul it out. She said Butch put the title in her name so the boatyard wouldn't give me a hassle."

"Did you?" he demanded.

"With what?" I laughed, "my Volkswagen? I told her to hire a commercial company, but she said they'd require a hull inspection for insurance reasons and Butch wouldn't allow it. She was supposed to clean out some compartment where he stashed dope for chick-parties . . . "

"Bullshit, bullshit, bull*shit*," Fred snapped back. "We'd built a watertight cubby hole to hide those plates! It would take an x-ray to find them. Where's Olga now? How is she living? Does she have money?" he probed.

"The last I knew she was in Houston with Jeff Baker," I shrugged.

Fred dropped his head into his hands and squeezed his temples until his fingernails went bloodless and white.

"Oh, God, oh God, we could be swimming in perfect bills," he groaned. "Now they're gone, they're gone . . . "

I sneaked a peek at the time. I had a little bit more than an hour before my cabbie was due. I began to feel a bit of pressure from the ever tick-tocking of time.

"Hey, didn't Meyer Lansky die in Miami back in what, '82, '83? I sure wish I could've met him just once."

Fred slowly lifted his head to press his lips against the rim of his now empty shot glass.

"January 15, 1983," he whispered while turning the glass round and round. "That man was the greatest genius of our time, y'know? He and Joe created the perfect laundering system. It was 99.9 percent bulletproof. Only eight people in the whole *world* ever knew how it worked and now there are two, maybe three of us left."

I sat as still as a statue, counting ten, fifteen, twenty, then thirty thudding heartbeats. I didn't say a word or even so much as release an audible breath, fearing it would bring back from wherever his thoughts were centering. Finally, after what felt like eons, he muttered, "Can you believe those bastards still have one of our archbishops penned up in the Vatican?"

My brain froze mid-thought. Where, oh, where had someone told me about high-ranking clerics being mixed up with the Mafia? Had it been Sturgis or Jake? I had to keep Freddy-baby rolling while I flipped through my memory bank.

"So who'd he tick off, Lansky or Bonanno?" I asked, refilling our glasses.

"I'm talking about the FBI. See, he was one of the key links to our loop." He paused for a moment then smiled, "It's funny, in a way. He and the other one were the only human beings on earth that could've pulled it off. One got our money out, the other sent it back in. In fact, Bobby, over the years, we flushed more money out of the States than you or I can count. I know it was over a billion dollars. The funny part was that we did it right under the nose of the IRS. Not only that, it came back as clean as new-blown snow.

"Know what we did then? We invested every dime into legitimate shopping malls, apartment buildings, condominiums and housing projects . . ." he trailed off for a moment. "Listen, this is the *real* touch of genius! We only held minority shares in any venture we bought into. Know why? When the Feds caught on, they couldn't separate our money from those rich boys who'd never spit on a sidewalk. We were untouchable. Pretty smart, huh?"

"Damned smart," I said and meant it.

"Hell, we even held millions in state and municipal bonds," he smirked. "How respectable is that?"

"And that's why Harris and Company got into all those malls around Tucson," I said. "But hadn't they started out in California?"

"Yeah, but when those twin jerk-offs got cocky, we moved them to Tucson so they'd be within tapping distance. See, we already owned the sheriff and a whole shit-load of politicians and judges. If only those Feds had stayed off our backs, we'd still be running Arizona and half of California."

Freddy-baby sighed and shook his head. "But none of it could've gone down

FROM MOSCOW TO EAST END REVELATIONS

had it not been for our archbishops."

Again with the "archbishop" routine. Was he testing me? I took the chance of switching subjects to see if he would switch back.

"Hold up, Freddy. Something's been eating at me. Was our film studio deal in Panama for real or was that Olga's carrot to keep this jackass," I said, gesturing with my thumb at my chest, "in line?"

"Yeah, it was 100 percent and we all could've made a bundle there, too. Hey, remember when she told you we'd only pay you for what you did there, but every film was 100 percent ours after we'd imported it? Know why we said that? We wanted to see if you'd dip your beak when you had your hand in our pockets. But, if you'd played us straight, we'd have given you an extra taste down the line. Trust me, we always know how to appreciate team players," he smiled knowingly.

"Yeah, but that never happened, so how did I screw it up?"

"It had nothing to do with you, for chrissake. We had to put that on the backburner until we could get a fair shake with Torrijos. Get this, that beanbag had the balls to demand that we let his brother run your studio so they could dip their beaks into our pockets while dicking every wannabe actress in town. When we gave up and told him to screw off, the dumb bastard froze all the money we'd stashed in his bank." He snorted, winked, and growled, "We got every freaking cent back after he took his last plane ride." I knew, of course, that Fred was referring to the explosion on August 1, 1981, where El Presidente's aircraft exploded midair. I wasn't sure, from his tone, if he was implying the explosion was of their doing.

"I got to say this, Fred, hanging out with you was never boring." I smiled at him. "But what you said a minute ago about archbishops and a billion dollars sounds like a movie script. I know you're just making fond memories more alluring. I know that couldn't have been for real."

"No, it really was. Know what? Screw it. It's all over now anyway," he said despondently.

"Oh, great!" My sarcasm was deep. "Thanks a lot for leaving me hanging!"

I took a turn pouring shots. I tossed mine, but Fred sipped and sighed, sighed and sipped until he sucked in a long, wet breath.

"Look, Bobby, the hardest part, and it wasn't *that* hard, was getting our money out of the States. Getting money back was really a snap because we only used 100 percent legitimate brokers out of Spain and the Caribbean. We made it look like foreign capital was coming in to invest. Better yet, we only bought into legitimate ventures where the Feds would never expect us."

"Was that why Olga kept jetting around?"

"Yeah, but she only delivered instructions to our brokers. Beyond that she knew zilch," he assured.

Another glance at the time warned me that my witching hour was closing in fast. I rolled the proverbial dice again and prayed for snake eyes.

"Look, I won't sleep for a month wondering, and I'm asking only because *you* say the game is over. How in hell did you use *archbishops* to get past the IRS?"

Fred snatched up the bottle and poured three overflowing rounds. I scored one, my socks got two.

"Look, Morgan," he croaked, "Paul Marcinkus is one of those archbishops. In fact, he was top of the list."

"Who's he?" I asked.

"He's the son of a Russian window-washer who'd brought his family to Cicero to chase the great American dream. The local gang of kids tried to put the new boy in his place until big Paulie had busted a few heads. Instead of sticking shivs in him, they made him a gang-member so he could help carve out their turf.

"Later, when those same ginnys got old enough to join their fathers' game as made men, they cut him [Marcinkus] out since he wasn't Sicilian. He had to make a choice. He could wash windows with his old man, he could take a dead-end job in a factory, drive a truck or maybe a taxi, or become a priest. Marcinkus took the collar."

"That must have really shut him down with his old buddies," I snorted.

"Don't be a schmo," he snorted back. "They made him their go-to guy whenever they'd pull some shit and felt the need to save their rotten souls. Can you imagine how he felt watching those crum-bums duked out in tailored silk

FROM MOSCOW TO EAST END REVELATIONS

suits with gold cufflinks, tooling around in flashy cars with bimbo broads hanging on each arm?" Fred shook his head. "I guess another light went on. He knew if he stayed just another parish priest, he'd end up with a prayer book in one hand and a whacked-off shlong in the other. That's when he got smart and took a blood oath with his dago pals that he'd be their man 100 percent if they'd pay his way into one of those Vatican colleges. So, they greased the right palms and off he went. But Marcinkus knew that one day they'd call in their chips for that favor. Now, guess what smart-boy does when he gets there? He cozies up with another priest named Montini who was a closet faggot."

(Giovanni Battista Montini reigned as Pope Paul VI from 1963 to 1978. Insiders considered him to be an active homosexual. If so, he may have been drawn to the virile Marcinkus, who would not be above using this attraction to its fullest advantage. This could explain Marcinkus' meteoric rise to power.)

"You mean Marcinkus went homo?" I gasped.

Fred laughed and splashed more booze in the general direction of our glasses. His didn't last ten heartbeats; mine hit my shoes.

"No," Fred replied, "but Paul had figured this Montini character had a better-than-even shot to become the next pope. He also knew there would be a shit-load of backstabbing along the way. So, he appointed himself Montini's protector. It was the smartest move he ever made. His buddy not only made the 'Big Chair,' he named himself Pope Paul VI! Get it? Pope *Paul*! I'm sure Marcinkus loved that. Better yet, he made Marcinkus his personal bodyguard and executive assistant.

"Paul knew his power would last only as long as Montini lived, so he started digging up all the dirt he could find on everyone and everything. Later on, he whispered to the Pope that he suspected some hanky-panky might be going on at 'the Vatican Bank' [Banco Ambrosiano]. When his buddy granted him unlimited access, Marcinkus burned the midnight oil until he'd recorded every Vatican investment around the world. That made him 100 percent untouchable."

"Bloody brilliant," I said and, again, meant it.

"Morgan, do you believe in pre-destiny?" Freddy-baby asked.

Funny question considering I had once asked myself something very similar that started this roller coaster. "The jury is still out on that one. What does that have to do with anything?"

"See if you can explain these 'coincidences' any other way. See, Paul Marcinkus had no clue that Meyer and Joe needed the Vatican Bank as their key link to smuggle out The Commission's millions. Understand? How could Marcinkus know they had already financed a clean family guy in Chicago to get control of the exact same bank its archdiocese was using to transfer its tithings to Rome? Are you following me?"

"Yes, sure, but why Chicago?" I asked.

"Are you kidding? Some of the wealthiest Catholic churches in America are in Illinois. Besides, Bonanno heard Archbishop Cody kept an expensive mistress on the side to play his sex games. Joe sent someone over to snap a few pictures of their action and sent him [Cody] some samples. The deal was Cody could play ball or his bare ass would be plastered across the front pages of every rag sheet in town. Cody got smart in a heartbeat."

(John Patrick Cody was Archbishop of Chicago from 1965 to 1982 and was elevated to Cardinal in 1967. Cody's years in Chicago were riddled with federal investigations about his personal financial improprieties. He also had an improper relationship with one Helen Wilson for period of twenty-five years. It was alleged that he provided her large sums of money to purchase a grand home, a luxury car, expensive jewelry, clothes and furs, etc. Several millions of dollars of church funds were discovered missing while Cody was treasurer of that organization. The Vatican suspended its half-hearted investigations upon Cody's death in 1982, a death that "coincidentally" occurred only months before Meyer Lansky died.)

"OK, but how did Joe and Meyer hear about Marcinkus?" I prodded.

"I'd guess his name came up from the boys in Cicero when they were setting up Cody. Joe and Meyer must have been damned happy to learn that mob money had put Marcinkus exactly where they could use him."

"Freddy, that's absurd," I snorted. "If I wrote any of that into a screenplay, nobody would believe it."

"No doubt," he agreed, "but that's exactly why we slipped so much past those schlemiels at the IRS. Hey, do you remember those newspaper headlines about Bonanno disappearing around '64? Even the cops figured he'd been

FROM MOSCOW TO EAST END REVELATIONS

dumped in some lime pit. That was a crock! He was gone over a year before he popped up looking like a million bucks. Nobody with half-a-brain swallowed that yarn about his cousin locking him up in his basement in Buffalo, but who could prove otherwise, right? In truth, Joe had been in Milan setting things up between Marcinkus and Roberto Calvi . . . "

I interrupted. "Calvi? Wasn't he that banker they found hanging under a London bridge a few years back?" I queried.

"Yeah, but when Joe first met him, he was about to lose his kneecaps to some Sicilian gambler. Joe bought his debt and from then on his ass was ours."

"Why him?" I asked.

"Why, the man asks!" he snorted. "Because Calvi was first in line for the exact position Joe needed at Banco Ambrosiano to complete our pipeline! Remember, he already had that banker guy in Chicago ready to wire Cody's tithings that included our piggybacked money to the Vatican Bank where Marcinkus was always waiting. He would deposit the righteous tithing into Cody's account so his records matched the Vatican's to the nickel."

I thought about that for a moment. Religious organizations were exempt from taxation, so the IRS didn't spend a lot of time investigating monies sent to respective parent organizations. If a pre-planned scheme had been arranged to easily identify what belonged to the church, legitimately, to carve out of what was riding piggyback, it was an easy and communications-free plan. The IRS didn't audit, the result at the Vatican matched the books the church maintained . . . he was right; it was virtually flawless when kept covert.

"Where did your money go?" I asked, after the full scope of the idea had seeded itself in my mind.

"Paul zipped it over to Banco Ambrosiano where Calvi scattered it out through a maze of pass-through accounts that Meyer had set up all over Europe. Then he'd use our shell companies to get it to the investment brokers."

I kept prying. "Olga said you had one in Venezuela."

"We had more than one and more in the Bahamas and the Caymans," he elaborated.

"Why so many?" I asked, eyebrows furrowed.

"We were playing a sort of shell game. Let's say Meyer wanted to invest into some mega-mall or a hotel in Arizona. He'd use maybe a half dozen of his shell companies to provide the money through brokers in different places. That way if the IRS looked at who owned what, they'd get a list of what appeared to be small-time investors. So where's the red flag? Remember what I told you; we never took controlling interest in anything."

I nodded. "That part I got, but how could you slip a billion dollars to Rome if you only used Chicago as its source?"

"We didn't need more operators; the fewer the better. OK, follow me and you'll understand. Let's say Cody was about to wire a righteous $125,000 for one month's tithing. We tack on a single zero. Understand? Do it once and you'll catch on."

I dipped my finger into the dregs of my whiskey and drew 125,000 on the table. He reached over to add a zero making it $1,125,000. That one digit added a full million dollars.

"See what I mean? No matter what Cody had, we rode piggyback."

"And then what happened?"

"When that wire came in, Marcinkus deposited the righteous amount in Chicago's account but zipped our money over to Calvi."

"I see," I said. "And if anyone crosschecked what the Chicago bank had transferred against what had been credited, the numbers would match to the penny."

"Bingo! You've got it. See how simple that is?"

"Whew! So how did you keep all this straight?"

"That had been my dad's [Morris Kerr] job until I took over. And to balance our books, all I had to do was match what went out against what came back minus what we paid Paul, Roberto, our banker in Chicago, and the usual fees the interim banks and brokers charged. We were able to keep anywhere from 80 to 90 percent for investments."

"How often could you pull it off?"

"Anytime the churches in that diocese had a cake-bake or a fair or any anything that raised a dollar for the Pope, we'd hop a ride for whatever that extra

FROM MOSCOW TO EAST END REVELATIONS

zero could give us."

"Did any of the other Vatican accountants get wise?"

"Oh, they knew something was going on every time Paul locked the door to his office. Remember now, the Pope's pet gorilla was a loner and no one dared stick their nose in his business."

"Then it all came down," I sighed. Of course, I was the one who knew why.

"Yeah, but look what happened after it all fizzed out. Even the FBI got reined in because they couldn't separate our interests from the civilian investors or they'd put them all into bankruptcy. Know what they got from us? Less than *half*! The other half went right making us bread," he bragged.

"Can't deny it, man, you put together one slick operation. Slick, slick! Maybe you and I should make a movie about all this. I've been working with this French buddy, Sergio, and he'd be just the guy–"

Freddy-baby erupted. "Jesus freaking Christ, Morgan! With Joey and Marcinkus still alive? We'd both end up under bridges like Calvi!"

"OK, OK!" I calmed him, putting my hands up in a mock shield. "You can't blame me for thinking . . ." I noticed my watch. "Whoa! Look at the time. My taxi's probably waiting. Early flight, you know. Thanks for dinner. I'll call next time I'm coming through," I offered, getting up.

"They murdered him, you know," he whispered.

I stopped mid-turn. "Who murdered who?"

"Morgan, I'm a human being and I have feelings just like you. But what they did to that honest and humble man haunts me. No, *he* haunts me. He was the only one with guts enough to stand up to Marcinkus. He only wanted the truth. Who gave those son of a bitches the right to murder a saint on hallowed ground? Even now, no one knows or cares about it. What am I supposed to do, let his killer get away with it?"

I was completely baffled. "Whoa, my man, who are we talking about? Who got murdered?"

"*Pope John Paul*, who else? It's been what . . . ten, twelve years?" he asked, squinting an eye with the effort of the thought. "But I still get sick when I think about it. I've tried to forget but I can't and I never will. Maybe that's why God is punishing me? Maybe that's why I'm penned up in this greasy hellhole.

"But, Bobby," he sobbed, "Bobby, I can't stop thinking about him and it's driving me nuts!"

Damn! I had but a few minutes before my trusty cab driver was due. I heard a muffled cough from somewhere in that smoke-filled darkened room. A hand flutter reminded me that Fred's wife was still between the door and me. What if his China doll had a pig-sticker in her garter belt or a meat cleaver stashed under her chair? Damn, damn, double damn! Even every piece of silverware had disappeared when our table was cleared.

Well, I still had our last liquor bottle.

Kerr's voice snapped me back to attention.

"Do you know what really happened to Albino Luciani?"

"Er, who?" I asked, thoroughly confused.

"Pope John Paul I! He's was the Pope for thirty days before he died."

"Oh, right!" I agreed, "Didn't that happen some ten or fifteen years ago?"

(Luciani was pope from August 26 to September 28, 1978.)

"Did you know he'd signed his own death warrant when he ordered a raid on Marcinkus' office and confiscated his confidential records?"

"Um, no. But what's that got to do with–"

"Everything!" he roared. "Unplug your ears! Look, it's hard enough to accept the connection between that holy man's death and Meyer and Joe's operation with that lunatic Marcinkus. John Paul had been pope for what, one stinking month. I'll admit that for years I kept myself in denial and didn't want to accept the obvious, OK?"

"OK, OK, Fred. So why does that upset you now?"

"Look, I never minded the money-shuffle and all that, and yeah, I knew the Mafia was up to its ass in blood, OK? But I never expected them to murder a pope!"

His speech quickened and his words ran together; it was as if he was afraid to stop. That was OK with me because I didn't want him to stop. I leaned forward to stare into his eyes, as a good listener should.

FROM MOSCOW TO EAST END REVELATIONS

Indeed, Fred went on to describe how the Vatican had elected to cover up the murder of their pope because any response to the contrary would have invited a million inquiries about their secrets, secrets they must conceal or risk losing the faith of the faithful. After all, how much more would their parishioners donate once they learned their archbishop was using their tithings to keep a mistress while helping the Mafia smuggle their ill-gotten gains through the Vatican's own bank? On the other hand, how about that high-and-mighty archbishop Marcinkus who not only had both hands in their pockets, he'd helped to murder their pope!

I paused to listen while he described how the Vatican had chosen to whisper that a heart, weakened by chain smoking, had caused Pope John Paul's unexpected death. Reports also claimed he was a closet alcoholic, another contributing factor.

None of it was true, of course, Fred swore. "Dig him up," he said, "take tissue samples and I'd take any odds that he'd either been poisoned or we'd find a needle prick in his neck."

I sat still as ice and waited.

"That's not the end," Fred said. "Roberto Calvi's turn came next. They found him hanging beneath [London's] Blackfriars Bridge sometime in '82. They tried to make it look like some secret Masonic organization had killed him and faked his suicide."

"Was it? Faked, I mean?"

"Maybe you know, Morgan," he accused half-heartedly. "Maybe you're someone I never really knew. Like I said, our sweet deal began falling apart right after Olga brought you to us. Why were you always there to help pick up the pieces? Now you're here. Am I next?"

Freddy buried his face in his hands to sob and shake.

"You go now," She-Lee whispered in my ear.

The distance to the door seemed endless. I wondered what or who awaited me, if anyone. Perhaps my cabbie had forgotten or had taken another fare. Before I even made it to the door, my self-protective voice kicked in with the "what if" this and "what if" that. I turned the door handle, half expecting to find it locked. It wasn't. I twisted it and stepped onto the landing only to see London's most beautiful cab and its best damned driver waiting below. I scrambled down, two steps at a time, to leap in atop my neatly folded Burberry.

The closer Jaime and I came to the lights of London the more my stomach unclenched and the more I wondered if my precious Emily was, at that very moment, tucked in for the night. I sent her another phantom kiss and wondered if she might sing our favorite bedtime song as she slipped into slumberland.

Years later, I was told that John Charles Piazza III had been given the name "John Petracelli" and placed in the Federal Witness Protection Program. His dearly purchased freedom was short-lived; because in his arrogance, he returned to his old gangster games. He was sent back to prison and placed in a special wing reserved for inmates who were at risk for their lives—not from the guards, but from their fellow inmates. Indeed, there was a hefty reward placed on his head by other Mafia members and there was no shortage of fellow "lifers" who would have gladly killed him so their family could claim that reward.

I also learned that Olga Elias spent a few years in Houston living with Jeff Baker. However, their merry life with easy money vanished. Jeff was disbarred and the last anyone knew of him, he was earning his bread playing piano in bars.

As for Frederick Kerr, some folks in the States claimed he had succumbed to another series of heart attacks. Each time I pass through London I think about calling the phone number on his business card. But I don't.

In some ways, I have pity for them all—until I remember that deal that went down at the schoolyard.

May God bless and protect the little children.

AFTERWORD

SUMMARIZING THE MAFIA AND THE VATICAN

From the attempted assassination of Pope John Paul II, to finding Roberto Calvi's body hanging beneath Blackfriars Bridge before he could be brought to trail, to known Mafia gangsters being granted burial in Vatican-owned cemeteries, the history tying the Vatican to the Mafia is too well documented to be ignored or denied.

In 2005, the tie became even more viable. An anonymous caller, later identified as the son of a member in a ruthless Rome-based Italian criminal organization called Banda della Magliana, revealed that the body of a long-missing teenage girl had been secretly buried in the crypt of prior Magliana boss Enrico "Renatio" De Pedis. De Pedis has the bizarre honor of being interred at Sant'Apollinaire Basilica in Rome alongside bishops and cardinals. In 2010, the Vatican finally approved for De Pedis' tomb to be opened.

Reports had claimed that the teenager, Emanuela Orlandi, had been kidnapped to use as a bargaining tool in favor of releasing Mehmet Ali Agca, the Turkish gunman responsible for the attempted assassination of Pope John Paul II in 1981. Other reports state that the fifteen-year-old girl was kidnapped in an effort to silence her father, who worked at the Vatican and may have stumbled on records tying the Vatican to the Magliana family. Some even speculate that the girl was taken on the orders of Catholic Archbishop Paul Marcinkus, central to part of this story.

Perhaps we will know sometime soon. At the time of this writing, the tomb was slated to be opened in 2011.

WHERE ARE THEY NOW?

Robert W. Morgan currently lives in a small, quaint skiing town in northern Montana where he dedicates his time to write fiction and nonfiction books and film scripts. He occasionally accepts speaking engagements at colleges and universities.

Frederick Coward, Jr., now retired from the FBI, lives in Hawaii, and owns and operates an international investigative firm, ISI Corp. His firm serves clients including U.S. and foreign government agencies, multi-national firms, banks, pharmaceutical corporations, technology firms, and more.

Norman Jones, also retired from the DEA, leads a quiet suburban life playing golf in Arizona and helping to support the Dubliner Bar.

Frank Sturgis died on Dec. 4, 1993, at the age of 68 in Miami, reportedly of cancer. He was plagued by accusations of involvement in the John F. Kennedy assassination to the day he died. He remained active in the formation of anti-Castro Cuban paramilitary groups and training volunteers in the art of guerrilla warfare. Morgan served as his adjutant and created PSYWAR manuals for his organization. Morgan was the only non-Cuban who stood honor guard at his funeral and acted as a pallbearer. Robert was further honored to ride in the family limousine.

Michael "Mikey Ducks" Centoducati vanished from Morgan's life.

Archbishop Paul Marcinkus served as president of the Vatican Bank from 1971 through 1989. He was credited with stopping an assassination attempt on Pope John Paul II in 1982 in Portugal. He resigned his post in 1990. Marcinkus remained safe inside the Vatican to escape all charges related to the scandal at Banco Ambrosiano and Roberto Calvi. After making a secret deal with the FBI, he was permitted to returned to the Archdiocese in Chicago in 1990, but retired to Sun City, Arizona, to be near his mentor, Joseph Bonanno. He died in 2006 of unknown causes at the age of 84.

Joseph "Joe Bananas" Bonanno died of natural causes on May 12, 2002, at the age of 97. After Bonanno's retirement in the 1980s, the Bonanno family was removed from the Mafia's commission after the leaders found out they were involved in drug trafficking, a violation of their rules. In 1983, the long-time Mafia boss wrote his autobiography, A Man of Honor.

Meyer Lansky, whose real name was Meier Suchowljansky, died in Miami on Jan. 15, 1983, at the age of 82. He suffered from bad health from the 1960s until his death and had been hounded by the feds for much of his life.

ABOUT THE AUTHOR

Robert W. Morgan is a charismatic loner who currently lives near the snow-covered peaks of Whitefish, Montana. Morgan, an astute patriot and loving father, spends his life in pursuit of his passion for filmmaking. Always involved, he is in close touch with his daughter regardless of any physical distance that may be between them.

He recently published two nonfiction books and recorded CDs through a division of Idyll Arbor Press. In 2009, he and several media professionals formed The Talisman Media Group, LLC for the purpose of producing feature motion pictures and creating a theme park near Glacier National Park.

Morgan speaks publicly and remains vocal about his beliefs. He actively encourages everyone he meets to live life to the fullest but to do so with character and heart.